What People Are Saying About *A Beautiful Life*

* * *

"What a powerful reminder of what really matters—loving God and loving people! Kerry Clarensau reminds us that *A Beautiful Life* is the result of allowing the example of Christ to overflow in our hearts so that it impacts every person we meet. The discussion questions are ideal for small groups, and the message of this book is a must for every woman who longs to leave a legacy that outlasts her life."

CAROL KENT

Speaker and Author, Unquenchable: Grow a Wildfire Faith that Will Endure Anything

"I love this book! Through powerful Scriptures and profound personal stories we glimpse the personal life of the author and her close friendships. She eloquently reminds us how to love others with style and grace. Oftentimes we don't consider love as a powerful catalyst. This book challenges us to use this catalyst to fight battles, set boundaries, forgive those who have hurt us, and be a better friend in all our relationships. Love is a choice we make; an action word as Kerry teaches us. When we love like Jesus, through selflessness, we will wake up one day and be able to say we too have *a beautiful life.* Thank you, Kerry, for writing this book with excellence. Every person who is in relationships of any kind will be better for it."

SHEILA HARPER

Founder and CEO of SaveOne (an international abortion recovery ministry)
www.saveone.org

"Kerry Clarensau has done it again. This gifted leader has written yet another great book that is sure to inspire, encourage, and challenge every person who reads it! In a world tainted with ugliness, most of us long for more beauty in our lives. *A Beautiful Life: Discovering the Freedom of Selfless Love* takes us back to God's original design for how life can, and *should*, be lived. Kerry uses relatable personal stories woven together with biblical truths to show us that beauty in life isn't something we acquire from having pretty things around us or having perfect circumstances. Instead, a truly beautiful life comes from having God's love *within* us and pouring it out freely to those around us in the context of healthy, selfless relationships. Come to think of it, that last sentence describes my friend, Kerry, to a beautiful T. If you long for a life of lasting beauty and freedom that makes a difference to those around you, this book is for you!"

JODI DETRICK, DMIN

Author, The Jesus-Hearted Woman: 10 Leadership Qualities for Enduring & Endearing Influence
www.jesusheartedwoman.com
www.jodidetrick.com
ICF Certified Coach, www.significantlifecoaching.com

"If you have relationships, this book is for you! Kerry Clarensau gives an outstanding relationship blueprint from the pages of God's Word. When we allow God's love to flow through our lives, broken relationships are restored and freedom is found! I'm thrilled that you've chosen to pick up this book. As you engage this journey, I'm certain you will walk away with new hope, greater faith, and the courage to dream again!"

RUTH E. PULEO

Director, Women of Purpose
www.penndelwomenofpurpose.org

"Across this planet women are searching for role models and relationships that are genuine and life-giving. They are looking for women who have an unwavering passion and commitment to pursue their purpose and are willing to share their life journey to strengthen and encourage those around them. Kerry Clarensau is such a friend and role model to me. As a wife, mom, and leader (in ministry), she continually inspires and challenges me and thousands of others to rise up and be all God has called and created us to be. Through her girlfriend-next-door style, her personal stories, and her incredible ability to teach God's Word, I promise she will captivate your attention. But, most importantly, the words in this book will motivate you to be more like Jesus and will compel you to love the people in your world just as He does!"

DEBBIE LINDELL

James River Church, Lead Pastor, James River Women and Designed for Life Director
www.jamesriverchurch.org
www.designedsisterhood.org

"Excellent authors weave deep psychological truths with simplicity and clarity that is both thought-provoking and enjoyable to read. Kerry Clarensau is one such author. In *A Beautiful Life*, Kerry magnificently weaves scriptural truths with healthy psychological principles in a manner that is delightful to read, illuminating, and life-changing. Kerry's latest book is a must read for those who desire more love, joy, and richer relationships!"

DR. MELODY D. PALM

Licensed Clinical Psychologist
Director of Counseling & Psychology, Assemblies of God Theological Seminary

"This book will change the way you think about love. You may think you are a loving person, you may feel you've tried to love others well. It may seem like others simply aren't returning the favor. But Kerry's message, spoken from a place of wisdom and grace, will open your eyes and your heart to what you've been missing all along. As you learn to practice real, sacrificial, restorative love, your friendships will improve, your relationship with God will improve, your marriage will improve, and you'll feel more filled and covered with love than you've ever felt before."

ALLISON VESTERFELT

Author, Packing Light: Thoughts on Living Life with Less Baggage

A Beautiful Life

DISCOVERING THE FREEDOM OF SELFLESS LOVE

Kerry Clarensau

Influence
RESOURCES

Published by Influence Resources
1445 N. Boonville Ave.
Springfield, Missouri 65802

Cover illustrations by Angela Moody and Shar Mavrich. © 2014 The General Council of the Assemblies of God. All rights reserved.

Cover design by Patti Long

Interior formatting by Prodigy Pixel

NOTE: Some of the names in this book, as well as some identifying details, have been changed to protect the anonymity of the people involved.

ISBN: 978-1-93830-995-3

17 16 15 14 ● 1 2 3 4 5
Printed in the United States of America

* * *

*This book is dedicated to the many women who
have inspired me to live a beautiful life . . .*

*First and foremost my mom, Helen—from the day I was born she
has been my up-close view of a woman who loves selflessly.*

*My mom's sisters—Janice, Fran, Linda, and Marilyn, who have
shown me what it's like to love one another deeply from the heart.*

*My grandmas—Edna Mae and Pernecia, who loved me
unconditionally from the moment they knew I was on the way.*

*My mother-in-law—Fran, who loves me and has
embraced me into her amazing family.*

*Friends and family who have taught me so much about
sacrificial love—Katie, Mindy, Michelle, Mickey, Becky, Jill,
Carol, Jodi, Peggy, Joanna, Debbra, Kristi, Laurel, Denise,
Darla, Jennifer, Alex, Karlene, Michelle, Carla, Lynda, Becky,
Kay, Ruth, Karen, Sheila, Debbie, and honestly so many more.
I hope you know who you are and how much I love you!*

*My life is so much more beautiful because of these amazing
women! I treasure each and every one of them.*

* * *

Contents

Foreword

T here are so many clichés, truisms, and cultural messages that drive our thoughts and ideas when it comes to love—it's no wonder we're all confused. We see Cinderella dance with her prince charming; we watch lovers in a movie race into the pouring rain to embrace in a passionate kiss. We wonder to ourselves, *Is this love? Are we missing it?*

I have been writing about marriage and family for three decades, and I have learned two important things about love. First, love is the most powerful force in our lives. It has the ability to change our whole reality, to alter our hearts, and change our minds. The love of Christ and the love of others is so powerful, nothing can rival it.

The second thing I have learned is a little bit more depressing: None of us know how to do it.

Love isn't easy. It doesn't come naturally. Something about love seems to go against our nature at times and certainly against our cultural training. We want love, but we aren't sure how to give love; therefore we're missing the most powerful aspect of it.

Is it possible for this to change?

Many years ago, when my grandson Michael was ten years old, he came to me in a crisis. I answered the door to the sound of his desperate knock and, when I opened it, I found him crying. He was completely out of control, trying to explain what had happened. I could hardly understand a word he said.

This wasn't totally out of character for Michael. He was always looking for adventure, and once he got an idea in his head you couldn't deter him from it. Whether it was having lightsaber wars in the living room or shooting fireworks in the garage, once he set his mind on something, there was no distracting him.

Although this frustrated me at times, I have always been deeply committed to each of my grandkids (I have ten), and I will do anything to help them. So I invited Michael inside and the two of us sat in my study. I reassured him and reminded him how much I loved him. After a few minutes, he calmed down and was ready to talk.

He told me about something that had happened with his mom (who happens to be my daughter). This wasn't the first time something like this had happened. They had a tendency to butt heads.

I asked him what specifically was bothering him, and he gave me the list. She had too many rules, too many chores, too strict a schedule for activities and homework. He wanted more freedom to do things his way.

"She's driving me crazy!" he said.

I let him talk until he was finished, and then I interjected.

"Is this the way you want to live?" I asked.

"No," he said, "it's not."

"Do you want to give your mother the power to control the way you feel like this?"

He looked at me, dumbfounded, and silently shook his head.

"Do you notice something different about how I'm acting right now?" I asked. "Different from the way you are acting?"

"You're calm," he replied.

"Yes, and do you know why I'm calm?"

"Why?"

"Because I have learned the secret of staying calm, even when life seems turbulent. Even when I'm angry, upset, or frustrated, I have a secret ingredient that keeps me calm."

He tilted his head a little and squinted his eyes.

"Do you want to know what it is?" I asked.

"Sure." he said.

"Love."

I went on to explain how he could join me in this great adventure, if he wanted to discover the counter-intuitive, counter-cultural, life-shifting power of love. He could manage his emotions, simply by controlling his thoughts throughout the day. If he meditated on love, I told him, this could all change.

He didn't totally understand, but he could see a glimmer of hope in me and, by faith, he trusted.

I pulled out my Bible and flipped it open. Together, we wrote down five Bible verses, and he promised to meditate on them and memorize them. Some of those verses were Romans 5:3–5. They go like this:

> "We also glory in our sufferings, because we know that suffering produces perseverance; perseverance, character; and character, hope. And hope does not put us to shame, because God's love has been poured out into our hearts through the Holy Spirit, who has been given to us."

We talked about how his relationship with his mother felt like a huge hardship. I helped him see how a hardship could become perseverance. That perseverance could turn into character, which would ultimately produce hope. I asked him if he'd like to have God's hope, so he could see his relationship with his mom, not as a problem but as a gift.

He agreed, emphatically.

When he left that day, he was in much better spirits. He agreed to memorize the Bible verses, which I promised to memorize with him. He put five stones in his pocket and carried them around everywhere as a reminder to memorize those verses. Within a few weeks, he had the verses memorized and was waiting for his love for his mom to grow.

Have you ever been in a circumstance like this—where you want to love someone, but you just can't seem to feel it? Maybe you have reminded yourself that love isn't a feeling, that it is a commitment to a person over a long period of time, but the longer you try to love someone who drives you crazy, the less interested you become in loving or serving that person.

Love can be challenging. It can be confusing.

A few weeks after my conversation with Michael, his relationship with his mom again became tense.

One afternoon, as she drove him home from school, she asked him where his books were. Suddenly, he realized he'd made a mistake.

"Oh no, Mom" he said. "I left them at school in my locker! We have to go back. I have a spelling test tomorrow, and I haven't studied yet. I need those books."

In that moment, she became angry.

"Michael," she said sternly, "it would be one thing if this were the first time you had forgotten your books, but this is easily the tenth time this has happened this year. What am I going to do with you? You're so irresponsible! When are you going to take your schoolwork seriously? I don't know what to say!"

She lectured him for another few minutes, getting more frustrated all the time. He simply let her finish. As she talked, all he could think about was Romans 5:3–5 and how this conversation was an opportunity to experience God's *character* and *hope*.

When she stopped talking, Michael said, "Mom, you're right. In fact, I want to thank you for your lecture because what you say is true. I haven't been the best student I could be this year. I could do so much better. I'm learning, slowly, but I'm thankful you care about me enough to be honest with me. God is using your words right now to bring me all kinds of gifts. I'm so thankful for that."

As he said these words, he felt the hope and peace of God pour love into his heart.

His mom stopped in her tracks. In fact, tears started flowing down her cheeks, and she had to pull the car over to the side of the road so she didn't get in an accident. Once she was safely off the road she asked: "Where did *that* come from?"

Michael told her about his conversation with me, about the Bible verses, and about the stones in his pocket. He told her how he had prayed for God to bring love into his heart for her, even though he didn't like all her rules. He told her God was answering that prayer, and he was starting to see her as a gift.

She cried and cried, stunned at the courage and maturity of her young son. And just like that, love changed their lives.

Later that day, Michael ran over to my house to tell me what had happened.

"Grandpa, grandpa!" He exclaimed. "It worked! Today was the greatest day of my life!"

Love changed the trajectory of Michael's life in that moment. It changed him, it changed his mother, and it changed the way the two related to each other.

Michael is twenty years old now, and he is a powerhouse for God. Like the verse in Romans promises, the hardships he suffered certainly produced character in him, as well as hope. That hope shines through now in every aspect of his life because Michael was willing to take a risk on love.

Perhaps you can identify with Michael. There is someone or something in your life that makes it difficult for you to love. It's stealing your hope, your happiness, or your joy. You want to love. You want to believe it's possible—but you aren't sure how. Just as my grandson was willing to step forward in faith and follow my example, will you step forward in faith and follow the example of my friend Kerry?

You won't regret it. The best and most beautiful days of your life are ahead.

GARY SMALLEY

Best-selling author and speaker; family counselor, president, and founder of the Smalley Relationship Center

By Design

• • •

Y ou were designed to love and be loved. Did you know that? You function best when you are loving and being loved. Think about it. When your relationships are at their best— when you have friends who love and support you, when you're working as a team with the people at work, when you and your family are enjoying and learning from each other—my guess is you are clear-headed, productive, and happy.

On the other hand, consider how you feel when your relationships are strained. When you argue with your husband, have a stressful morning with your kids, or have a dispute with your coworkers—how does that affect you? Do you feel tired? Scattered? Out of sorts? We've all been there.

The first three chapters in this book discuss how we are created to love and to be loved. As we look together at Scriptures and even some scientific research, I believe you'll see how love is the most important thing in your life: love for God and love for others. And as you apply these principles, I also believe that, no matter your circumstances, you'll begin to experience more joy, more happiness, and more fulfillment.

Your life will truly be *a beautiful life.*

CHAPTER ONE

Created to Love

"But remember the root command: Love one another."

JOHN 15:17, MSG

I haven't always known relationships are the most important part of life. For most of my life, I thought work was the most important. Relationships were always fun and enjoyable for me. In fact, from the time I was a little girl, my favorite time of day was when the family came together around the table for dinner. But despite that feeling, I assumed *work* was the real substance of life and relationships were just the fun part.

This idea affected the way I ordered my life and went through my days. I worked long hours to be a good student, a great worker, and a good mom. I always wanted to be a high achiever and a hard worker.

Then, one day, my perspective changed.

I was busy at work, putting together a project I was determined to complete in record time. This material was going to be used for students from kindergarten through high school to learn more about the love and freedom found in Jesus. I was so certain God wanted me to do everything I could to make sure those students didn't have to live another day without the material. The harder I worked, the faster I worked, the better.

While I was working, I received a phone call.

On the other end of the line was my friend Carol, who had been walking through the most painful experience a mother can possibly face. Her sixteen-year-old son had been diagnosed with cancer, and after a long battle, had passed away. The minute I heard her voice I knew I needed to stop what I was doing and listen. As she poured out her heart, God spoke something deep into mine.

She told me that a few weeks before Josh had passed away, the family knew his remaining time on earth would be short. So they asked him how he wanted to spend his last few days. He said he wanted to spend time with the people he loved. As each one entered the room to say good-bye, he gave words of wisdom—far beyond his years—to each one.

To his grandpa he said, "Don't weep for me for very long, because where I'm going the sun is always shining, and I won't be in pain anymore."

To his friends he declared, "You better live right. I won't be here to grow old with you, but I want to see you again in heaven."

The family played worship music for him and read Scriptures at his request. He found the music and the words comforting as he suffered intense physical pain. After my friend recounted to me the last hours of her son's life, it occurred to me: When he knew life was about to end, young Josh cared about two things: his relationship with Jesus, and his relationships with others.

> At the end of our lives, the only thing that will matter is our relationship with God and our relationships with others.
> #abeautifullife

After I hung up the phone, I walked out of my office, leaving the half-completed project on my desk. My to-do list faded, the sense of urgency faded. I walked, slowly across the hallway and entered a chapel. I stood at the back for a few minutes— I'm not sure how long—then walked solemnly, slowly to the front. Eventually, I sank down in a pew, buried my face in my hands, and wept. I prayed: *"God, help me to love You and those You put in my life. Help me to remember the lesson that Josh's life proclaims."*

Maybe relationships are the most important thing, after all.

Love One Another

When you face your last days, will you wish you had worked harder or will you wish you had loved better?

Jesus knows we will wish we had loved better. I think that's why He spoke so often about love. The command to "love God" is found twelve times in The New International Version of the Bible, and the phrase "love your neighbor" is found nine times. In addition, more than forty New Testament verses contain the words "one another." These instructive passages teach us *how* to love each other well.

Since that life-changing conversation with Carol, it's become obvious to me that God really wants us to get this loving thing right. This is one of the things He cares about most.

John 15:9–12 says, "As the Father has loved me, so have I loved you. Now remain in my love. If you keep my commands, you will remain in my love, just as I have kept my Father's commands and remain in his love. I have told you this so that my joy may be in you and that your joy may be complete. My command is this: Love each other as I have loved you." I'm struck by the strength of that command. Loving others is not an option. God doesn't command us to "accomplish as much as we can;" He commands us to "love one another."

> WE FUNCTION AT OUR BEST, PERSONALLY, WHEN OUR RELATIONSHIPS ARE RIGHT WITH GOD AND WITH OTHERS.

We actually function best when we love others well. I hadn't considered this idea very carefully before I read Dr. Caroline Leaf's book *Who Switched Off My Brain?* But after reading her research, it makes perfect sense. Dr. Leaf's research shows that our brains are literally clouded when we don't love others well. We function at our best, personally, when our relationships are right with God and with others.

When you experience the love of God and of people, your heart speeds up its communication with the mind and body through your blood vessels. Life is in the blood, the body's transport system, and the heart is in charge of making sure the transport works.

Health travels from the brain to the heart in electrical signals and from there to the rest of the body.[1]

How amazing is that? (I *love* it). When we experience love with others, and the love of God, our blood transport systems actually quicken and our health improves!

This is a scientifically documented reality. Dr. Allan Schore, a leading researcher in the field of neuropsychology, has written extensively about our basic need from birth for love. More than food and water, from the minute babies come out of the womb they need to attach to a loving relationship.[2] This is it, dear friend. Love is the most important thing in our lives.

Is Love Missing?

As you're reading this, I wonder if you feel like love is missing from your life. Perhaps, as you read the research by Caroline Leaf, and the command from Scripture to "love one another," you nodded your head and thought, "Yes, I *am* at my best when my relationships with others are at their best, and when my relationship with God is right. When I experience love, I feel happy and healthy. That rings true to me." But I wonder whether you also thought, "If other people would do a better job of loving me, my life would be so much happier and healthier."

You're not alone in feeling that way.

I've felt that way myself, on many occasions, and in the many years I've spent encouraging women, I've met countless women who felt the same way. We instinctively feel that love is important, that it matters more than anything else, and that a lack of love might negatively impact our lives . . . yet we feel powerless to change our circumstances.

This was certainly how I felt before Carol called that day. From the outside, it looked like I had the perfect life. I had a great job, a beautiful family, and hundreds of friends. Yet my life lacked a commitment to love well, and I felt overwhelmed, burned out, and unfulfilled.

Your circumstances might be totally different from mine. Maybe you have parents who abandoned you or a husband who treats you as if you're worthless. Maybe you feel alone and isolated. No matter where you are, you can understand what I felt in that moment: You wish you had a deeper commitment to love. You want to love deeply; and be loved deeply in return.

I'm glad you're reading this book.

In the following chapters, we're going to explore how to get more love in your life, to fulfill who God created you to be. But it won't be what you think. You don't need another set of parents, or a different husband, or a brand new life. What you need is a renewed mind, heart, and spirit of love. And guess what? God can give these to you. It might seem impossible, but it's really not. Love is closer than you think.

●　●　●

"Life − love = 0."

RICK WARREN

CHAPTER TWO

Created for Joy

"I have told you these things so that you will be filled with my joy.
Yes, your joy will overflow! This is my commandment:
Love each other in the same way I have loved you."

JOHN 15:11–12, NLT

I think most of us know, instinctively, that we were created to feel and experience joy. When we have it, we want to stay in that place forever—to recreate our circumstances and experiences, just to get another taste of it. When we don't have it, we know something is wrong. We try to orchestrate circumstances—vacations, new clothes, a great job, a new title—to produce that feeling of joy.

What we don't realize is this: We experience true joy only when we allow the love of Jesus into our lives and we give that love freely to others.

Three years after my life-changing conversation with Carol, my husband and I moved to Wichita, Kansas, to pastor a great group of people. I had high expectations for the move and the new opportunities. I thought about all the things Mike and I would accomplish together and the kind of life we would lead. And while I had learned an important lesson from Carol about valuing relationships over accomplishments, I'm not sure the lesson had moved from my head to my heart.

Needless to say, things didn't turn out exactly as I had planned . . . yet God wasn't the least bit surprised.

To say I struggled in the transition is an understatement. Mike settled in right away and instantly began to make an impact in the community. I was miserable. Nothing was as it had been, or as I thought it would be.

In my previous role, I had worked with a clear job description and was constantly stretching and growing. I had developed curriculum, led a staff, traveled, did public speaking, trained leaders, and served on numerous national committees. I had grown into all of those "roles" over time and had enjoyed the challenge, busy schedules, and feelings of accomplishment.

Now, I was a pastor's wife—and there was no job description for that! Not only was I confused about what I was supposed to do, I felt lost without opportunities for growth and greater responsibilities. I was used to defined parameters, measurable goals, and firm expectations. This new role of serving alongside my husband was ambiguous, and I didn't like it at all.

In addition, I had lost a comfortable salary. My husband was making enough to support our family, but we had no cushion in our finances.

For the first year, I was completely convinced we had stepped outside of God's will when we moved to Wichita.

Isn't it funny how we do this—when we're put in a difficult or uncomfortable position, we assume we can't possibly be in God's will? What if, in the difficult seasons of life, God is refining us, teaching us, and ushering us into His peace, blessing, and joy . . . all in His perfect will?

During that difficult season, I spent hours on my knees. God's Word became my greatest source of comfort. Many days I felt I could only function if I spent time in His presence. During those times of prayer, He helped me see that I had attached my identity and my fulfillment to accomplishments and roles. Because I was striving so hard to achieve, my life lacked true joy.

WHEN WE TAKE OUR EYES OFF OURSELVES AND FOCUS ON JESUS AND OTHERS, HIS LOVE BEGINS TO FLOW THROUGH US.

One Sunday during a morning worship service, as we sang a song titled "Dwelling Places," one line stood out to me: "Jesus, my joy, my reward." In that moment, it hit me—*Jesus* is my joy and my reward. As long as I remain in relationship with Him, I can find everything my heart longs for.

The more I focused on myself in that difficult season (my role, my disappointment, my confusion), the more miserable I became. It *is* miserable to focus on ourselves. From that perspective, all we can see is what we wish could be different about our circumstances. But when we take our eyes off ourselves and focus on Jesus and others, His love begins to flow through us. Jesus really is our joy and our reward. We experience His love best when we receive it from Him and give it to others.

> If we love each other, and we love each other well, the result is going to be joy.
> #abeautifullife

Those words from that song meant so much to me that I designed them in a document, printed it, and put it in a beautiful frame. It stands on my dresser to this day.

God's love is powerful enough to fill all the empty, broken, and confused places in my spirit. Not only that, it's big enough to overflow to the people around me. I learned that no matter what season of life we are in, we have the opportunity to experience the joy of quiet moments with Jesus, and then to allow those moments to overflow to others.

Joy doesn't come from titles, positions, or accomplishments. It comes from receiving God's love and allowing that love to be the catalyst for absolutely everything we think, say, or do.

Finding Joy in Life

I'm not sure if you can identify with my story. Can you think of a time when you felt directionless or your life lacked fulfillment? Do you feel that way now? Perhaps you want to make more money so you can buy beautiful things or go on vacations. Perhaps you're single, and you feel life will get started when you're married. Perhaps you're a mother of young children, and you find yourself longing for your kids to grow up so you can do something fulfilling (trust me—the days might be long, but the years are *really* short).

No matter where your heart is as you read these words, I want you to hear this: Right now, God has you in a specific place for a specific purpose for a specific season. You don't have to wait for your circumstances to change or improve to experience true joy. The source of joy is not a bigger house, a better job, or more extravagant vacations (although at times it can seem like it!). God is the source of all joy. He is the giver of fulfillment and joy, and He invites us to be givers of fulfillment and joy *with Him.*

This is where we find a beautiful life.

If you want more joy—and more love—in your life, seek Him first. Ask Him to fill your life with His love the way He filled mine, and to help you bless others with the overflow.

Most of us intuitively understand that a life without joy is no life at all. We pray for joy, seek joy, and when we experience joy, we try to replicate it. But what if we're looking for joy in all the wrong places? What if the way to receive more joy and experience more joy is to *give* (and receive) more love?

That's what I think Jesus was talking about in John 15:11–12. It's no accident that Jesus says joy is linked to love. Without true love, you can't experience true joy.

❋   ❋   ❋

"A joyful heart is the inevitable result of a heart burning with love."

MOTHER TERESA

CHAPTER THREE

Created for Relationships

"For this is the message you heard from the beginning:
We should love one another."

1 JOHN 3:11

Although God created us to experience joy in relationship with Him and with others, I have to admit it isn't always easy to do. I'll never forget the season God taught me this truth.

Several years ago, Mike and I pastored in a small community. It was the first time I had lived in a small town. I had to get used to fewer people, fewer places to shop, and running into people I knew. Not only this, but our sons were young and I was staying home with them, so my whole life revolved around our small boys, our small town, and our small church family.

Each day, instead of going to work as I had in our previous position, I stayed home. I loved being a mom, and certainly found ways to keep busy, but I didn't feel I was as productive or "effective" as I wanted to be. Most of the day I wiped noses, picked up smashed Cheerios off the floor, or cleaned up accidents in the bathroom.

Then I met Becky.

Becky lived across the street and was a stay-at-home mom like me. She had two young children, and the rhythms of our lives were similar. I would see her out during the day, getting the mail or watering the flowers on her front porch.

One day, I decided to introduce myself to her. Becky and I became instant friends.

We began doing life together. We took the kids strawberry picking, went for walks, had picnics in the park, and talked over coffee or tea. We shared about our lives and what it meant to be a mom. I encouraged Becky when she was feeling discouraged about something, and she did the same for me. I invited her to visit a Bible study I attended, and we ended up going each week. That's where Becky committed her heart and life to Jesus.

We spent time together, and without much effort at all, my negative feelings about that season of my life melted away.

A year and half after we moved to that small Kansas town, our church denomination elected my husband to a position of leadership, which meant he would have to work at the district headquarters—in a different city.

We had to move again!

I couldn't understand why this was happening. I was thrilled for my husband and his new opportunity, but it didn't make sense. This wasn't part of our plan. We had planned to be in that little church for a long time. I couldn't understand why God would move us to a town for seventeen months and then move us away.

To make matters worse, the leaders at the church in Kansas were frustrated that we were leaving. They hadn't expected us to leave so quickly, and I can imagine they felt abandoned. I tried to remind myself that God's plans don't always make sense to us. I talked myself through the process. But the more frustrated the congregation and leadership became, the more I had to wonder: Had we heard God wrong?

I'll never forget the week we packed our things to move. Becky was over at our house. Her kids were playing with my kids, and she was helping me put some things into boxes.

"I don't understand, Becky," I told her. "Why would God bring us here for seventeen months and then move us away?" Becky paused. And what she said next changed my perspective of the situation completely.

"Kerry," she replied, "I think you moved here for me."

In that moment, it hit me: God loved Becky enough to send me and Mike to a brand new town, for only seventeen months, so she could know about His love. He loves her that much, He loves me that much, and He loves you that much. What a gift to be the hands and feet of Jesus to Becky for just a short time. I pray I will be His hands and feet wherever I go.

> THE MOST IMPORTANT, ENJOYABLE, LIFE-GIVING WORK IS CONSTANTLY AT OUR FINGERTIPS— LOVING OTHERS.

The most important, enjoyable, life-giving work is constantly at our fingertips—loving others. Becky helped me see that there are people all around us who need love, and when we give love, we receive ten times what we have given. God has made us for this. What a beautiful life!

It doesn't matter if you come into contact with someone for a few minutes, a few hours, a few months, or a few years. The opportunity for growing and enjoying relationships is universal. It's constant and continual.

> What if giving love is the most fulfilling thing you can actually do?
> #abeautifullife

The best part is that it's enjoyable! We are made for joy, and joy is a byproduct of love. The two are connected. That's why, when I reached out to Becky and shared my life with her, I received joy in return. The negative things I had felt about life melted away when I decided to enjoy a relationship with her. The change was truly beautiful.

I believe the same can happen for you!

Unexpected Fulfillment

We don't usually expect to feel full when we give something away. In fact, most of us, I would argue, want to hoard things, protect things, and keep things to ourselves so we don't face more emptiness. But what if giving love is the most fulfilling thing we can do? It's counter-intuitive, and definitely counter-cultural, but so are most truths found in Scripture.

Do you feel lost? Unfulfilled? Dissatisfied? Do you feel as if you're in a holding pattern, waiting for the next thing to happen in life? That's how I felt before I introduced myself to Becky—as if I had to wait for another time or other circumstances to feel fulfilled. Are you willing to consider the possibility that giving love to someone else would help you feel fulfilled and satisfied?

As the apostle John tells us, we've had the command to love one another from the beginning of time. The Christian life is not going to be easy, but it will be most fruitful, enjoyable, and beautiful when we live in community with each other.

The best part about looking at relationships this way is that it opens your eyes and your heart to opportunities to love and to find joy that are all around you. Perhaps you can walk with a friend, bake cookies for your neighbor, have coffee with someone who is hurting, or prepare a hot meal for a family in need. This is what life is all about—it's about relationships . . . about caring for each other.

I can already hear you protesting (mostly because I've thought and wondered some of these same things). What about those who mistreat me? Am I supposed to love them? What if I've tried to love others, but it hasn't worked? What if I feel like I don't have any love left to give? Don't worry. We'll tackle those issues in the next chapters.

* * *

"I would rather walk with a friend in the dark than alone in the light."

HELEN KELLER

Going Deeper
PART ONE—BY DESIGN

DISCUSSION OR JOURNAL QUESTIONS:

1. You are created to love. Read the quote from Dr. Caroline Leaf on pages 12–13. Discuss the difference in the quality of your life when you love others well and when you have no meaningful connections.

2. You are created for joy. "Joy doesn't come from titles, positions, or accomplishments. It comes from receiving God's love and allowing that love to be the catalyst for absolutely everything we think, say, or do." Describe a time when you experienced great joy because you showed someone the love of God.

3. You are created for relationships. First John 3:23 tells us, "For this is the message you have heard from the beginning: We should love one another." How does understanding that you are created for relationships help you invest your time, energy, and resources wisely?

A PERSONAL CHALLENGE

The author shared, "We don't usually expect to feel full when we give something away. . . . But what if giving love is the most fulfilling thing we can actually do?" Consider someone in your life who would benefit from something you have to give—time, energy, or resources. Show that person extravagant love this week. Consider journaling your thoughts through this experience.

PART TWO

Love Is Not Optional

· · ·

G od *is* love, and He reflects love. Everything beautiful in our lives comes from love. In order for us to be in relationship with God and to experience a beautiful life, we must learn to love in the way He loves. Love isn't simply a nice idea; it's a command from God that enables us to experience peace, fulfillment, and joy.

When we love others we are kind and gracious with them. This includes our family members (yes, *all* of them)—siblings, children, spouses, parents, and crazy Uncle Bob. It means we are kind and gracious to our friends, coworkers, and the people we interact with every day—waitresses and baristas. It also means we are kind and gracious to our enemies.

As Christians, it's easy to get caught up in the complicated details of our faith. But if we consider what Jesus taught, and the way He lived, the most important aspect of His teaching was this: *simply love.* In fact, Jesus tells us in Matthew 22:37–40, "'Love the Lord your God with all your heart and with all your soul and with all your mind.' This is the first and greatest commandment. And the second is like it: 'Love your neighbor as yourself.'"

CHAPTER FOUR

God Is Love

"God is love."

1 JOHN 4:8

When my son Tyler was four weeks old, I took him for his first well-baby checkup. As far as I was concerned, he was the most perfect baby in the world. I had spent all four weeks of his life just staring at him, drinking in the creativity of God reflected in my child. I couldn't believe how little he was—his toes, his ears, his lips!

The appointment started off routinely. The pediatrician weighed and measured him, and I waited expectantly, excited to see how much he had grown. The doctor looked in his eyes, his ears, and listened to his heart. Everything seemed to be looking good. But when he grabbed Tyler's legs and moved them in a circular motion (as doctors do in a baby checkup) a look of concern grew over his face.

"I would like to get some x-rays of Tyler's hips," he finally told me.

I almost melted to the ground. What was happening? Why would he want to get x-rays? What could this mean? My mind raced with a thousand possibilities and worst-case scenarios.

The pediatrician whisked Tyler off to get x-rays, and I waited, praying everything would be okay. When the pediatrician returned, however, he had the orthopedic specialist with him.

"Your son has congenital hip dysplasia," the specialist said nonchalantly. "It's rather severe. If this condition isn't corrected, he'll never be able to walk normally."

Everything the doctor said after that moment faded into the background, behind the spinning of the room and the beating of my heart. Tears poured down my cheeks as I struggled to watch them wrap Tyler's small body in a stiff brace. Everything about this seemed like a nightmare. It wasn't possible this was really happening, was it?

That afternoon, all I wanted to do was hold Tyler. It wasn't easy holding a baby in such a stiff brace, but I didn't care. Every part of my heart cried out for him and craved a way to protect him from the inevitable difficulty and pain he was going to face. As I rocked Tyler to sleep, I prayed for a way I could give Tyler my healthy hips, even if it meant taking his unhealthy ones.

I loved this precious baby so much. I was afraid people would make fun of him, that he would suffer physical pain, that he wouldn't be able to experience a normal life. Fear overtook me in that moment as I sat and rocked my baby. I wept and cried out to God.

"Please help me!"

In that quiet moment, God spoke something so clearly to my heart. He said, "Kerry, I love Tyler even more than you love him. And I love you more than you love Tyler." *How could that be? I wondered. I love Tyler so much. How could God possibly love him more than I do? There isn't enough love in the world for me to give my child.*

As I reflected on how much God loved Tyler, and me, an indescribable peace washed over me. I thought about the amazing connection between my desire to trade my healthy hips for Tyler's broken ones—and the way Jesus so selflessly sacrificed Himself on the cross for my sins. He loved me *so much* He traded His healthy life for my unhealthy one. He took my place.

> God's love is vast, immeasurable, enduring, and redemptive. He loves no matter what. We love because He loves us first.
> #abeautifullife

The love I felt for Tyler was a mere fraction—simply a reflection—of the love God has for us.

Tyler was in braces or a full-body cast until he was about twenty-four months old. He was also diagnosed with another type of dysplasia at the age of five and had several surgeries as a teenager. But today, Tyler—both a husband and a father himself—is as able-bodied as they come. He walks normally, runs, plays baseball, basketball and soccer, and generally enjoys an active life.

I wish it had not been necessary for Tyler to go through the pain of hip dysplasia, but I'm so thankful for the lessons we learned on our journey as a family. Sometimes God gave us just enough strength to face the moment. Other times He brought caring people to lend a hand. Once, He brought miraculous healing after months of swelling and pain from a surgery.

More than all that, loving my son through the pain of his hip dysplasia taught me about the love of God. When God looks at us, He doesn't see what we see. He doesn't see the scars or the defects—He sees His *child*.

Can you imagine the emotional pain for Tyler if he had somehow thought he had to overcome his physical ailment in order for us to love him? If you're a parent, you can join me in saying this idea is *ridiculous*. Yet this is how we often approach our heavenly Father—we assume we have to pull ourselves together and be whole before we can experience His love.

What if we simply trusted His love?

He loves us enough to cradle us—brace and all. He loves us enough to rock us to sleep, even as He weeps for our pain and brokenness. He loves us enough to intercede with the Father for us. He loves us enough to trade His "healthy hips" for our displaced ones, His sinless life for our sinful one.

That's how much He loves you. Do you believe that?

Love Transforms

Understanding God's love is important to every part of our lives—our relationship with Him, our relationships with others, our understanding of ourselves. It's so basic that we can't begin to live the Christian life until we first understand the fullness of God's love.

First John 4:8 says, "God *is* love" (emphasis mine) and John 15:13 says, "Greater love has no one than this: to lay down one's life for one's friend." First John 4:19 says, "We love because he first loved us." Love is the starting point, the ending point, and

every other point in between. In other words, it is the love of
God that reaches inside us and changes us from the inside out.
Only because of His love are we able to offer this life-giving love
to others.

Love is everything that matters.

Dr. Caroline Leaf, author of *Who Switched Off My Brain?*,
has done years of research on the impact of negative thoughts on
the human brain, and her findings show that there are only two
basic human emotions: fear and love.
Out of fear come anger, bitterness,
discouragement, dishonesty, stress,
and depression. Out of love come joy,
peace, patience, kindness, well-being,
and fulfillment.[3]

If we're living in fear, she explains,
we can't live in love. If we're living
in love, we can't live in fear. This is
exactly what 1 John 4:18 says, "Perfect
love drives out fear." It also rings true
in my story with Tyler. I started the
day of his checkup in fear, but ended
it in love. When fear was present, love couldn't be. Once love
crept in, fear was gone. The love of Christ taught me to love my
child. It changed my attitude, and ultimately brought healing and
redemption to the story.

> UNDERSTANDING
> GOD'S LOVE IS
> IMPORTANT TO EVERY
> PART OF OUR LIVES—
> OUR RELATIONSHIP
> WITH HIM, OUR
> RELATIONSHIPS
> WITH OTHERS, OUR
> UNDERSTANDING
> OF OURSELVES.

God's love changed me from the inside out.

If you're facing a difficult situation in your life right now, if
you're allowing fear to creep in, perhaps you think, *"Kerry, this is
easy for you to say. You have a happy ending to your story. Not me.*

My son is dying of cancer. My mother abandoned me. My husband is leaving." Although I can only imagine the pain you must feel right now, I want to encourage you. There were years and years when we didn't know how Tyler's story would turn out. Yet in those years of uncertainty and fear, Jesus taught us about His love.

Understanding His love builds our trust. Without this, living the rest of the Christian life will be impossible. Everything I suggest in this book will be impossible. You'll try to love but you'll come up short, and end up feeling used, abused, and depleted. Perhaps you feel like that right now. Let me encourage you: There's nothing wrong with you! You're just trying to love by your own power; and you can't love others until you first know the love of our heavenly Father.

I want you to know this: God's love is vast and immeasurable. It's unfailing. It brings redemption and endures forever. His love brings life and grace to our lives. He is the source of love. He loves us first so we can then love others. If you want to follow Jesus with your whole heart, and you wish you had more deep and meaningful relationships, love is not an option. The good news is, Jesus is the source of love, and He gives us everything we need to experience a loving and beautiful life.

• • •

"We sinned for no reason but an incomprehensible lack of love, and He saved us for no reason but an incomprehensible excess of love."

PETER KREEFT, *JESUS SHOCK*

CHAPTER FIVE

Jesus' Message
Is One of Love

"A new command I give to you: Love one another.
As I have loved you, so you must love one another."

JOHN 13:34

I knew the greatest commandment was to love others, but I didn't have an easy time living this way. Have you ever felt like that? I knew Jesus wanted me to love others and experience His love for me, and He had demonstrated His love to me in so many ways. Yet, when it came down to it, schedules, agendas, strategies, and responsibilities always seemed to get in the way of love.

While I was doing research for this book, I took a trip to Israel. I wasn't thrilled about going. I mean, it was an incredible opportunity, and I knew that. I *wanted* to be thrilled about going, but I had so many things on my mind and projects to tend to in my hometown of Springfield. I couldn't bring myself to feel completely present in the moment.

My mind was spinning. I had a book to research and write. I was responsible to lead a team of people at the office. I'd been traveling nonstop for the several weeks before the trip and was worried whether I'd given them enough direction to do their jobs well.

I'll never forget when the plane landed in Tel Aviv and my phone started making all the noises it does after an international flight—buzzing and dinging with new emails, text messages, and missed calls. I felt a heavy weight settle on my shoulders and took a deep breath. *God, what am I doing here? I should be in my office.*

Has something similar happened to you? Have you felt you needed to be in two places at once—like your daughter's dance recital and your son's baseball game, which happened to be scheduled at the same time? Have you felt torn between spending the holidays with different family members in different parts of the country? *Should I be here, or there?* Maybe you've been on vacation, but all you can think about is how much work you have waiting at home.

Little did I know when I arrived in Israel that God had me exactly where He wanted me.

I left the plane with my group, and found my way to our tour guide, who was waiting for us at baggage claim. His name is Marc, and he led us to the bus where he helped us load our suitcases and other belongings. Forty-five minutes after the plane landed we were all settled inside. I looked out the window of the shuttle bus and thought to myself again: *God, what am I doing here?*

That's when Marc's voice came over the loudspeaker. He said, "I want you to know you are here because God wants to spend time with you in this place." My jaw dropped. It was as if God had spoken directly to me in that moment. It was as if He had said: *Kerry, I'm not concerned with all the things you have to accomplish back in Springfield. Your team will be fine without you. I've got them in my hand. Your book will be fine, even if you don't work on it this week. The most important thing is that you spend some time with Me. I have some things to show you.*

Right there, on the shuttle bus, I experienced a moment of intimacy with God. He spoke to me like a husband to a wife: *I just want to spend time with you! Will you slow down for a second so I can share some important truths with you?*

> "Jesus didn't give us a systematic theology, but He did teach us how to love."
> —Marc Turnage
> #abeautifulife

Over the next several days, as we toured Israel, Marc shared facts and details about Jesus' life. Seeing the places in person was like experiencing the stories of the Bible all over again, with more weight and reality than I had ever felt before. I thought about all the passages of Scripture I had read dozens of times and reminded myself: they happened *here!*

One passage God brought to mind was the story of the adulterous woman the religious leaders dragged into the town square. Being in Israel made me consider what it was *really* like for her when they brought her, uncovered and exposed, directly out of her sinful act. I pictured Jesus shouting above the noise of the crowd, "Let any one of you who is without sin be the first to throw a stone at her" (John 8:7). In my mind's eye, I saw Him kneel to the ground and draw something in the sand.

I thought about God, getting down into the dirt with us, to write us a love letter. I thought about the crowds pressing in, taunting us and reminding us of our faults and failures, telling us how we "should" live. I thought about Jesus putting His hand up, calling off the criticism, and telling us, "Go, and leave your life of sin" (v. 11). This is how much Jesus cares about love.

Jesus was all about love. When He said the greatest commandment was to love, He meant it.

As I toured this place I "wasn't supposed to be," a country filled with lessons and history and tangible reminders of the Son of God, our tour guide, Marc, said something I'll never forget. He said, "Jesus didn't give us a systematic theology, but He did teach us how to love." I hadn't thought about it that way before, but the more I explored the country of Israel, the more I learned about the life of Jesus, the more I realized it was true.

If we're not getting this love thing right, we're not getting much right at all.

The Greatest Example of Love

If we want to learn how to love—and how to love well—we must look to Jesus. He is *the* example. During His life here on earth, He had many demands for His time. When He traveled with His disciples, hundreds of people followed Him, came to meet Him, stopped Him in the street to ask Him for help. I don't know about you, but I might have felt overwhelmed by all those expectations.

Yet, unlike me, Jesus didn't feel overwhelmed by these requests. He didn't feel like He wasn't living up to some arbitrary expectation if He didn't meet those requests. Most of all, He didn't allow His destination or objective to get in the way of loving and helping others. He knew exactly what His Father had called Him to do, and He did it with conviction and strength.

He wept with Mary and Martha. He fed five thousand. He touched the leper. He healed the blind. He restored a crippled man's shriveled hand. He washed the feet of His betrayer. He asked John to care for His mother. He offered grace to the woman caught in adultery, and, of course, He offered forgiveness to the sinner hanging next to Him on the cross.

> IF WE WANT TO LEARN HOW TO LOVE—AND HOW TO LOVE WELL— WE MUST LOOK TO JESUS.

As I walked in Israel, I thought how Jesus, if He were on earth in our time, wouldn't be distracted by theological arguments or pressures to "be somebody" who mattered. He wouldn't be coerced by the culture to stay busy and accomplish as much as possible. He knew exactly what He was supposed to do and exactly who He was. He was God, and His job was to love people.

Consider the implications for us. No matter where you are today—if you're the busy working mom, or a woman caught in some type of sin (haven't we all been here?)—God wants to reveal something to you today: His message is one of love. He has no condemnation for you, only love. His requirement of you is simple: *just love.* His promise to you in return is simple: *If you will let Me, I can give you a beautiful life.*

You don't need to figure out the theology of Jesus in order to do life with Him. You just need to accept His love. You don't need to fill your schedule with accomplishments or accolades in order to impress Him or anybody else. You just need His love. You need to experience His love, and you need to share His love with others.

In fact, it is precisely by showing love to others that we show our love to Jesus in return.

•   •   •

"'Love the Lord your God with all your heart and with all your soul and with all your mind.' This is the first and greatest commandment. And the second is like it: 'Love your neighbor as yourself.'"

JESUS

CHAPTER SIX

Our Love for Others Reveals Our Love for God

"By this everyone will know that you are my disciples,
if you love one another."

JOHN 13:35

I knew it was important to treat others with respect and care, but this was made clear on my trip to Israel. That's when God reminded me that the way I treat others isn't just something I do to be a "nice" person. The way I treat others—my coworkers, my friend, my barista—reflects how I feel about God.

One day on our tour, we visited the road that links Jerusalem to Jericho—the scene of Jesus' famous parable of the good Samaritan (Luke 10). I'm guessing you've heard the story. A man is left, beaten and bruised, on the side of the road, and a kind passerby helps him to a hotel and tends to his wounds. This story has become so well-known, it's moved beyond Christian circles and into popular culture.

Good Samaritan is a term we use to describe a person who helps those in need.

The most remarkable part about this parable is not simply that one human stopped to help another human who was in need. The most amazing part of this story is that it was a Samaritan who stopped to help a Jew. Samaritans and Jews often didn't even speak to one another, let alone take care of each other.

Although I had heard this parable many times before, as Marc retold the story to us that day, I heard it in a brand new way. What had once been simply words on a page suddenly lifted into real life for me, and I began to think how amazing it was that all the people who should have stopped to help this man didn't. And the one who was the most unlikely candidate did.

When we ignore needs we're equipped to meet, we aren't just ignoring our brothers and sisters. Our treatment of those people reflects how we feel about God.

Jesus calls us to have faith like a child. What would a child do? A child would do the same thing Jesus did, the same thing the good Samaritan did: give love *beyond* what is deserved without judgment or expectation of return. This is the kind of love that brings about true change. It's the kind of love that draws us to Jesus, and the kind that will draw others to Him.

Before we left the Jericho road, Marc said something that made the whole lesson come together for me. He said, "I'm a parent. And being a parent, I know the fastest way to love me is to love my children. I also know the fastest way to make me angry is to mistreat my children." He paused for a minute before finishing. "I think God feels the same. I believe all of us need to think more carefully about how we treat God's children."

As he spoke, the words sank deep into my heart. I knew
he was right. As a mother myself, I knew exactly the feeling he
was talking about. I also knew I was guilty of treating others
in a way I would never want to
treat God. Would I speak to Jesus
the way I speak to my husband?
How about the way I speak to the
irritating telemarketer who calls
my house just as we sit down to
dinner? What about the cashier
who overcharges me? What about
the woman who takes forever in
the line at the grocery store?

What if righteousness
is as much about
rightness with
others as it is about
rightness with God?
#abeautifullife

Would I whine or complain? Would I distrust? Would I
harbor bitterness and disrespect? Would I be so controlling? If
the way I treat others truly reflects how I treat Jesus, maybe I
should examine how I treat others.

Reflecting the Love of Christ

After returning from Israel, I told friends about my experience.
I wanted everyone to know the shift of heart I had experienced;
and I wanted others to experience it, too. It wasn't that my
life had been absent of love before—it hadn't—but the more
my knowledge about love shifted from knowledge that was
"out there" in the world, to knowledge that was in my head,
to knowledge that I experienced in the depths of my heart, the
more real and beautiful and joyful life became.

I felt like someone had let me in on an awesome secret, and I wanted to whisper that secret down the row.

Have you ever considered that the way you treat others is a reflection of how you feel about God? Is it possible that the strain in your relationships is keeping you from a thriving, satisfying relationship with Him? If this connection truly exists, no wonder we feel out-of-sorts when our human relationships are strained. No wonder God cares so much that we get this loving thing right. When we snap at our husbands, belittle our children, or disregard a friend in need—we reflect disrespect and disregard for God.

You might be protesting right now. You might be thinking: *That's nice for you, Kerry, but you have no idea about the people I have to put up with in life. They're bullies, manipulators, mean, and basically impossible to get along with. My coworkers lash out at me for no reason. My mother is rude and controlling. My kids don't respect me. And don't even get me started on my husband . . .*

> HAVE YOU EVER CONSIDERED THAT THE WAY YOU TREAT OTHERS IS A REFLECTION OF HOW YOU FEEL ABOUT GOD?

If those are your thoughts, I want to encourage you: a beautiful life of loving God and loving others is possible. There's a difference between loving people and allowing them to use or abuse you. I'll talk about that in later chapters. For now, rest in the hope that it *is* possible to change your reality by changing the way you love.

I can't lie and tell you it will be easy. But no matter how toxic the people in your life can be, you can end the cycle. You have the power to choose how you respond. This might mean ending a relationship or setting better boundaries. (I'll talk about this more in future chapters.) But when you embrace your power to love—even those who don't deserve it—your anger, frustration, and bitterness will melt away. There's no room for fear anymore! All the space for fear is taken up with love.

When you choose to do this, out of obedience and love for God, your capacity for love will grow, your joy will grow, and your life will be transformed (even if slowly) into a beautiful life. When you love people, you watch them transform in front of your eyes. When you love people, you reveal your love for God and this fills your life with joy.

I hope you will join me for the next step in our journey.

•   •   •

"I see God in every human being. When I am tending the leper's wounds, I feel I am nursing the Lord himself. Is it not a beautiful experience?"

MOTHER TERESA

Going Deeper
PART TWO—LOVE IS NOT OPTIONAL

DISCUSSION OR JOURNAL QUESTIONS

1. God is love. He reveals His love to us in so many ways. Read Psalm 139 and discuss the ways God's love is revealed in the message of this chapter.

2. Jesus taught us to love. He wept with Mary and Martha. He fed the five thousand. He touched the untouchable. He healed the sick. He washed the feet of His betrayer. He asked John to care for His mother. He forgave the sinner hanging next to Him on a cross. How does His message of love challenge you specifically today?

3. The author shared the tour guide's challenge, "I'm a parent. Being a parent, I know the fastest way to love me is to love my children. I also know the fastest way to make me angry is to mistreat my children. I think God feels the same. We need to think more carefully about how we treat His children." How would you interact with the people in your life if you clearly saw them as God's children and really understood His love for them?

A PERSONAL CHALLENGE

This week, intentionally see every person you meet as a child of God who is dearly loved by Him. Ask yourself how He would want you to treat them. Consider journaling what God reveals to you.

PART THREE

The "One Anothers" in Your Life

. . .

Several years ago, I wanted to see exactly what Jesus had to say about love in the New Testament. In addition to the many commands to love God and each other, there are dozens of passages about how we are to treat "one another." These verses call us to live in harmony with "one another," forgive "one another," and bear "one another's" burdens—among many other things.

These verses became affectionately known to me as the "one another" passages. I studied them closely and began implementing the basic principles in my life. I shared them with the women in my office, my husband, my daughter-in-law, and my friends. I wanted to spread the word about what I felt God was teaching me.

In sections one and two, I shared with you some of the reasons I believe love is so powerful, and invited you to see how your life can change if you learn to be a conduit of God's love. I've talked about Jesus's example of love, and urged you to see how God cares more about how you love than almost any other aspect of your life!

You may be wondering how on earth this love thing works. Practically speaking, in real life, what does it look like to live a life full of love? This section, and the ones that follow, will help you uncover and practice love in your life.

I'll share some personal stories and a few stories from my friends, but the most important story for you to think about as you read is your own story. As I share from my experience, I encourage you to ask yourself: *How can I love others better?* God wants you to get this loving thing right. He's inviting you to live a beautiful life.

CHAPTER SEVEN

We Need a Variety of Relationships

"Live in harmony with each other. Don't be too proud to enjoy the company of ordinary people. And don't think you know it all!"

ROMANS 12:16, NLT

As God taught me what it looked like to love better, one of the first things He showed me was how important it was for me to have a variety of relationships. It was easy (or at least fairly easy) to love people who were like me, but loving those who had different backgrounds from me, were in different stages of life, had different temperaments, or whom I didn't understand was much more difficult. It took a conscious choice and putting my own interests aside to love these people.

When I chose to love those who were different from me, and allowed them to love me, my life became more beautiful.

A few years ago, my husband and I went to a restaurant in our hometown quite often. Most of the time, we had the same server. She was a young woman who, we learned over time, was a single mom. She was different than me—more different than anyone else in my life at the time. She was younger, a different ethnicity, had a different education, and a different family background. She wasn't a Christian. I don't know that we would have been friends if we had met outside of that setting. After all, we had nothing in common.

But she had a bold personality you couldn't ignore.

I'll never forget the first time she came up to our table. "Ya'll better hurry up 'en order," she said. "I ain't got all afternoon." Then, she cracked a smile that was so bright it could have lit up the whole room.

That's how she was—blunt and honest in a way I envied. She didn't filter her thoughts, she spoke loudly and confidently, and she asked a million questions. Over the few years we went to that restaurant, I fell in love with her.

Her laugh was contagious. She thought about things I never would have thought about. Her questions made me consider things in a brand new way. Every time I was with her, she helped my perspective. God taught me through the beautiful relationship I developed with this woman that sometimes the people we wouldn't choose as our friends (or siblings, or coworkers, or in-laws) are the very people God wants to use to help us become more like Him.

> IT ISN'T UNTIL WE LOVE THOSE WHO ARE DIFFERENT FROM US THAT WE SEE THE POWER OF LOVE TO USHER US INTO A BEAUTIFUL LIFE.

Something powerful happens when we intentionally love those who are *different* from us in one way or another (different stage of life, different experiences, or different personality). We see the transforming power of love at work. Our working relationships become more productive and life-giving. Our marriages and friendships flourish and grow. Our relationships with family members become deeper and more rewarding.

All across the board, our relationships get better. Our life becomes more beautiful.

The Gift of Variety

Chances are you gravitate toward people who are like you. You want to be around people who share your faith, your income bracket, your life-stage, your same interests, and even your neighborhood. In some ways, this is normal. Shared experiences build friendships. But in other ways, if we fail to love those who are different from us, we miss out on the beauty, joy, and fullness of life God has to offer.

Loving those who are exactly like us is fairly easy. It isn't until we love those who are different from us that we see the power of love to usher us into a beautiful life.

Jesus cultivated intentional community with men and women who were different from Him—from different backgrounds and walks of life—in order to come together and share life under the banner of God's love.

Picture the disciples. Here were a few working-class fishermen, a tax collector, and a zealot, all brought together to learn from one another and to follow Jesus. The early church went on to continue this example.

I don't know what the relationships look like in your life, but I know it's easy to fall into a routine of comfortable relationships. There's nothing wrong with these relationships, but they definitely limit our rapport with a diversity of people. Do you spend time with people who are different from you? If you answered no to that question, don't feel guilty. Let it encourage you to embrace those around you who are different, so you can give and receive the beauty of God's love.

> It is in relationship with those who are different from us that we are ushered into the fullness of life God has for us.
> #abeautifullife

You can and will be impacted by all kinds of relationships. Don't limit yourself to just one type! Relationships with people with special needs bring us back to the basics of human need and our reliance on one another. Relationships with the elderly teach us to slow down, listen to stories, and connect with our history. Relationships with family members who are difficult or critical teach us to have grace for others and grace for ourselves. Relationships with those who have walked away from God give us opportunities to be salt and light.

If you see gaps in your relationships, I want to encourage you not to wait for someone to make the change for you. Take responsibility to make it yourself.

If you aren't mentoring anyone, ask God to bring someone to you who could benefit from your time and energy (believe me, you have something beautiful to offer!). If you don't have a mentor, think of someone you could ask to take that position in your life. If you're not ready to ask for a full-time mentor, simply look for someone you respect who is ahead of you on the path you want to walk and invite them to coffee or lunch. Ask questions, and listen.

As you seek to develop a variety of relationships in your life, you'll be pleased to find they each meet different needs and bring different values. They'll each grow you and stretch you in different ways. Watch as the transforming power of love sweeps over and through and across your life. Prepare to be amazed at the graciousness of God demonstrated by others. I wish I could hear your story!

●   ●   ●

"I'm so thankful for friendship.
It beautifies life so much."

L. M. MONTGOMERY, *ANNE OF AVONLEA*

CHAPTER EIGHT

Whom Has God Placed in Your Life?

"Each one of us needs to look after the
good of the people around us,
asking ourselves, 'How can I help?'"

ROMANS 15:2, MSG

W e all have people in our lives who drive us crazy (if you're in a small group, don't look to your right or left). You know the kind of person I'm talking about. Someone who seems to cause drama in every circumstance, who constantly takes your words out of context, who is consistently negative and critical, who makes every minute you're with them miserable.

There are times when we need to draw a boundary around toxic people in our lives (I'll talk more about boundaries in Part Nine of this book). But there are other times when it's possible to love people right where they are—no matter how difficult they seem. This is *not* easy. It takes a strong person to love a challenging personality. But what if love could change that person from the inside out? What if love could be the one thing they need? What if giving that kind of love could change you, too?

Several years ago I was challenged to love someone who was really difficult to be around. I was leading a small group of about thirty women. Every Friday night they came to my house, and we ordered pizza or made tacos. We sat on the couch, ate food, and studied the Bible.

I was young in ministry and full of energy, so I spent a long time preparing what to share with these women. But every single week, the same thing would happen. The women came, they got their food, they sat around the room, and twenty-nine of them listened intently. The other woman was a complete disruption.

She interrupted me while I tried to teach, she interrupted other women when they tried to respond to my questions, she stirred up drama and started fights, and every time she spoke she projected loudly and directed the attention back to herself. It was miserable for everyone involved.

Honestly, my first response was to ask her not to come anymore. After all, wasn't her presence preventing the ministry that could be done with the rest of the women? Her behavior was erratic and irrational. She even had the potential to be dangerous, didn't she? It's amazing how quickly we begin to justify a solution that pushes people away, simply because they're inconvenient.

Immediately, as these thoughts entered my mind, the Holy Spirit convicted me. I felt God assure me I didn't need to ask her to leave. He reminded me that she needed my love and encouragement more than any other woman in that group. "I brought her here so you could love her," I felt the Lord say. I took a deep breath. "Okay," I whispered back, "then You'll have to help me do it!"

From that day forward, it was my mission to love this woman through her brokenness. It happened supernaturally. When God brought her to mind, I prayed for her. She attended that small group faithfully, and I found private times to talk with her about right and wrong behaviors for engaging others. She started contributing to the conversation in healthier ways, and when she did have one of her outbursts, God gave me the grace to see her as a child—a woman who had clearly been wounded at a young age.

> What if the most frustrating people in your life are placed there for a reason?
> #abeautifullife

Slowly, the other women in the group became more comfortable with her as well. The more accepted and loved she felt, the less she acted out. The less she acted out, the easier she became to love.

Just as the situation took a really positive turn, my husband and I made the decision to move away from the city. Late one evening, someone knocked on our front door. As I approached the door, I heard sobs on the other side. It was this woman, and she was weeping.

My first thought was that something tragic had happened with her family. She usually put on such a tough face and tended to have a sharp edge—I had never seen her broken like this. I ushered her into the house, through the entryway, and into the living room. As I helped her onto the sofa, she quietly said, "You *can't* move! You're the only person who has ever loved me."

While I had struggled to love this woman in my own strength, God's love had flowed through me to her in significant ways. Her life was transformed, and my life was transformed. Neither of us would ever be the same.

This experience taught me an incredible lesson—when we pray to love someone, God gives us everything we need to love them with His love. It's one of the most important prayers we can pray. We receive His love freely in order to give it freely.

Loving the Unlovable

Consider the people in your life. Some of them are easy to be around. Others are more difficult. Some are in your life for a long time (your parents or siblings), others come into your life for a period of time (a professor or a boss), and still others come into your life only briefly (a barista or the person next to you in traffic). What if each one of these people is placed there intentionally—both for their good and for your own?

> WHEN WE PRAY TO LOVE SOMEONE, GOD GIVES US EVERYTHING WE NEED TO LOVE THEM WITH HIS LOVE.

God is in every detail of our lives. He orders each of our steps. How precious is that? If you take this to heart, it can transform how you treat the people in your life. You'll begin to see that each person is designed by God, and even if they've been altered by circumstances, they're still made in His image. Even if they seem rude, even if loving them seems inconvenient, God has something to teach you and show you when you learn to love them as He does.

It's amazing to me how easy it is to despise difficult people in our lives. Yet, what if Jesus has led them to us for a specific reason? What if He wants to reveal His love to them through us?

As I mentioned before, loving difficult people isn't easy. In fact, it might be easier to push them out of our lives, ignore them, or wait until they go away. But if we do this, we miss out on the work God wants to do in our hearts and in theirs. If you're dealing with difficult people in your life, here are some things to think about.

TAKE TO GOD WHAT IS GOD'S. Sometimes we experience frustration with difficult people because we expect them to affirm us, fulfill us, or love us in a way only God can. For example, if you're frustrated with someone in your life because that person is critical, ask yourself why you take their words to heart so easily. Ask God to give you a clear picture of your circumstance, in spite of their harsh words. Ask Him to reveal your true value and worth, and where you have room to grow. When you stop expecting something from them they aren't able to give, you'll be able to love them genuinely.

PRAY. You can't love anyone in your own strength, and some people are so difficult we don't even *want* to show love to them. Ask God to give you the strength to love people in the way He loves them. When I did this, God taught me to see people as children. This isn't about looking down on someone but simply about seeing a person in their purest, most vulnerable form. Most difficult people are simply hurting, angry, grown-up versions of wounded children.

ASSUME POSITIVE INTENT. Most people, most of the time, are doing the best they can. Assume this about the people you encounter. When we look at people this way, it helps us respond in a positive way to even the most negative behavior.

AVOID NEGATIVE BEHAVIOR TO CONTROL OTHERS. Tactics like shame, manipulation, control, or anger can be effective in the short run, so they're the ones we turn to most quickly. But manipulation and control only make the situation worse. The goal is *not* to control the behavior of those you encounter, but to love them in spite of their behavior. Let God do the rest.

*   *   *

"When we are no longer able to change our circumstances we are challenged to change ourselves."

VICTOR FRANKL

CHAPTER NINE

Widows, Orphans, and Foreigners

"He defends the cause of the fatherless and the widow, and loves the foreigner residing among you, giving them food and clothing. And you are to love those who are foreigners, for you yourselves were foreigners in Egypt."

DEUTERONOMY 10:18–19

So far I've talked about what it looks like to diversify the relationships in your life, to notice who God has brought into your life—no matter how difficult they are. But the final chapter in this section is perhaps the most important discussion about the people God calls us to love. This is a given aspect of the Christian life: We are to love the orphans, foreigners, and widows.

I always knew God's command to love the orphans, widows, and foreigners, but I wasn't sure how to live this out in my everyday life.

When I began to study the "one another" passages, I also began to ask God to show me examples of the orphans, widows, and foreigners in my life. I'm still learning, and God has shown me others who fulfill this command in a beautiful way.

One example is my friend Jessica. She was flying home one night through the Atlanta airport where she met a young couple—I'll call them Alex and Gaby. Jessica noticed Alex and Gaby because she overheard them talking and recognized their accents. She had been to Iran several times and was sure that's where they were from. When they had a question about the flight being delayed, they asked Jessica for information, and this started a conversation.

Jessica asked where the couple was headed, and they said Branson, Missouri. The plane was flying into Springfield, Jessica's hometown, which is about forty miles from Branson. When she asked Alex and Gaby what they were going to do in Branson, they explained they were coming for the summer to work at a hotel restaurant.

> Everyone is to carry their own load, but sometimes they have loads they can't carry alone. Bear one another's burdens.
> #abeautifullife

Jessica, Alex, and Gaby boarded the plane, and sure enough, they sat right next to each other. Without even blinking, Jessica knew this was a divine meeting.

"How are you getting to the hotel when we land?" Jessica asked, as the flight neared its destination.

"We plan to take a cab," Alex answered.

Jessica was concerned. What Alex and Gaby didn't realize was that, since they were landing so late in the evening, it would be difficult and very expensive to take a cab to Branson.

Since Alex and Gaby didn't have any extra money, Jessica started brainstorming other ideas. Finally, she decided to call the hotel where they were employed to see if the manager would send a shuttle. He agreed, but said it would be several hours before the shuttle could be at the airport. Jessica had to leave— she had committed to bake a cake at her church that night—but the airport was shutting down, and she refused to leave this young couple outside, alone, in an unfamiliar location. So she brought them with her.

She put two perfect strangers in her car, and drove them to church.

Once at the church, her husband offered to give the two a tour of the building while she took care of the cake. As he walked them around, they noticed a small inscription on the wall that said, "Whatever you do for the least of these, you do for me."

Later, as Jessica drove the couple back to the airport to catch the shuttle, Alex asked about that quote. "Is that in your Bible?"

"Yes," she responded. "It is."

Jessica kept in contact with Alex and Gaby over the next several months. She visited them in Branson, and told them if they ever needed anything from her, she would love to help them. They had meals in her home and spent significant time with her family. When it came time for them to return to Iran, they called to tell her that their flight was leaving from New

York, but they had no way to get there. She helped them get all the necessary travel documents and a flight to New York.

Jessica and her husband took vacation time to drive Alex and Gaby to catch their flight out of St. Louis, paid for their baggage with Jessica's frequent flier miles, and made sure these young Iranians had everything they needed before she sent them on their way.

Her family invested time, energy, and financial resources in complete strangers from another country. Later she told me, "If these had been my kids in a foreign country, I would have wanted someone there to do this for them." I don't know about you, but I find her story inspiring. The love she showed to this young couple reminds me of the extravagant love God offers to us each day.

It occurs to me, as I think about Jessica's story, that each person has incredible value in the eyes of God. As she loved Alex and Gaby, God's love was demonstrated in a real, tangible way.

Why Orphans, Widows, and Foreigners?

I don't know about you, but sometimes I find it easy to go through my day without paying much attention to the needs around me. Other times, I notice a need, but I don't take the time to meet it because I don't want to sacrifice the resources; or because I don't want to get wrapped up in a problem that "isn't mine to solve."

Can you identify with this? Have you ever felt a nudge to engage someone, but chose not to (like the last time you traveled on an airplane and just wanted to take a nap)?

Jesus stands up against this mentality. He says the reason you are blessed is to be a blessing. The reason you have a platform is to stand up for others who don't. The reason you have money is to share. The reason you have access is to open it to others. My friend Jessica is an excellent example of what that can look like in real life.

Everyone is required to carry their own load (I'll talk about this more in later chapters), but sometimes we have loads that are just too heavy to carry alone. In this case, we're called to bear one another's burdens. We're called to look for needs, and innovate ways to meet them. We're called to treat others as we would want to be treated.

> EACH PERSON HAS INCREDIBLE VALUE IN THE EYES OF GOD.

Jesus cares deeply about justice and has a heart for the weak and marginalized. He's pleased when, like my friend Jessica, we go out of our way to help those in need. When we reach out to love those who have less than we do—who have real, tangible needs—we demonstrate the love of God and usher in the kingdom of heaven.

Now that's a beautiful life!

* * *

"The only reason for influence is to stand up for those who have no influence."

RICK WARREN

Going Deeper
PART THREE—THE "ONE ANOTHERS" IN YOUR LIFE

DISCUSSION OR JOURNAL QUESTIONS

1. We all need a variety of relationships in our lives. Read the description of the types of relationships on page 56. What type of relationship do you feel is currently missing from your life? How can you intentionally invest in that type of relationship?

2. Who has God placed in your life? What if the most frustrating people in your life are placed there for a reason? Read through the ideas on pages 63–64 to help you to deal with difficult people. How can these steps bring a healthy perspective?

3. We should defend the cause of the widows, orphans, and foreigners. Rick Warren said, "The only reason for influence is to stand up for those who have no influence." What would it look like for you to open your eyes to the needs around you?

A PERSONAL CHALLENGE

Carefully consider everyone who is a "one another" in your life—family, coworkers, friends, and neighbors. In your journal, write the name of each person and what each one is adding to your life. (Remember, difficult people can teach you as much as enjoyable people.) Then consider what you bring to each of them. Express your appreciation for someone specifically this week.

PART FOUR

Love Is a Verb

• • •

There are many misconceptions about what love is and how it works. Perhaps this is why we have found it so difficult in the past to love our neighbors as ourselves.

My hope is that, in the next three chapters, I can uncover some of the myths you've believed about love, and convince you that love isn't a thought or a feeling. It's an *action*. In fact, God is the ultimate source of love, and the ultimate demonstrator of love, and He "demonstrates his own love for us in this: While we were still sinners, Christ *died* for us." (Romans 5:8, emphasis mine). He demonstrated His love in Christ's death.

In another Bible passage about love, 1 Corinthians 13:1, Paul says something significant: "If I speak in the tongues of men or of angels, but do not have love, I am only a resounding gong or a clanging symbol." In other words, talking about love, proclaiming love, sharing love on Facebook status or Twitter feed is not the same as showing love.

If love is determined by what you *do*, how are you doing with loving your neighbor? Your check-out clerk? Your husband? When was the last time you *did* something loving for each one of them?

If love is an action and not a feeling, that changes everything. It means love is something we choose and control, not something that happens to us. It means that hate is not the opposite of love, as we so often think. Indifference is. Many of us (myself included) are guilty of refusing love to others, not with vengeful thoughts but with a sense of disinterest.

The goal for us is to open up our hearts to give and receive more love. It might seem challenging—and in some ways it is— but mostly, it's wonderful. Remember we were created for this. We were designed to love.

When you start *living love,* you begin to live a beautiful life.

CHAPTER TEN

Feeling vs. Obedience

*"Now that you have purified yourselves by obeying the truth
so that you have sincere love for each other,
love one another deeply, from the heart."*

1 PETER 1:22

I don't know about you, but I don't always *feel* like loving others. When someone at church says something hurtful to me, I *feel* like biting back. When my husband is short with me, I *feel* like being short with him. When the cashier at the grocery store says something rude to me, I *feel* like telling her manager about her poor customer service. But the Bible says we are called to love, even when we don't feel like it. In fact, love that exists only when we *feel* like loving isn't love at all.

Several years ago this practice of loving when I didn't feel like it was put to the test in my life.

My friend Sonora and I had known each other for many years when she deeply hurt our family. We were close. We had worked together on a few projects, spent time together weekly, and even talked about what life would be like when we were still friends, far into the future. But one day she did something that broke my trust.

Honestly, I was devastated. I felt betrayed, and I missed her company. To make matters worse, I realized that she was talking to our other friends about the conflict, spreading unfair information about what really happened.

I tried not to think about it, talk about it, or blow it out of proportion, but my anger and hurt feelings grew. I refused to gossip about it, despite the temptation to defend my family's reputation. Each time I saw her, these awful feelings surfaced in my heart, but I would smile, and tell myself to be nice.

During that time, I read and taught Tom Holladay's book *The Relationship Principles of Jesus,* and I'm so glad for this timing. Tom gives practical advice about love and forgiveness that really helped me through the conflict with Sonora. It's extremely difficult to show someone love when you don't *feel* like loving them at all.

> I LEARNED THAT IT'S OKAY TO TAKE MY "UGLY" FEELINGS TO GOD AS WELL AS MY "PRETTY" ONES, WHICH MADE MY RELATIONSHIP WITH HIM DEEPER AND MORE REWARDING.

Tom says that sometimes we think we're being hypocritical when we act loving without feeling it, but we aren't—we're being obedient.[4]

This was so helpful for me with Sonora. I was hurt, yes. I was angry, yes. I felt betrayed, yes. But my negative feelings toward her didn't mean I didn't love her. It meant I was hurt. I could be hurt and still *choose* to love her. I needed to *act* loving toward her, in spite of my feelings. I needed to take those negative feelings to Jesus, and treat her with love instead.

Loving her didn't mean I downplayed what she had done to hurt me, or that I excused her negative behavior. It just meant I gave good to her, even though she had given me evil. It meant I asked God to heal the hurt I felt, and I worked to control my thought life.

In this case, I didn't confront her with my hurt feelings. (I'll talk more about when and how to confront an offense in Part Six.). Instead, I did what Jesus instructs in Matthew 5:44, "Pray for those who persecute you." God gave me the grace to love her in spite of my feelings toward her, and in spite of her negativity toward me and my family.

The positive result was uncanny and unexpected. Not only did my feelings toward Sonora heal, but it kept the drama to a minimum among my friends. I learned that it's okay to take my "ugly" feelings to God as well as my "pretty" ones, which made my relationship with Him deeper and more rewarding.

Does It Really Work?

Some of you might be skeptical right now. You might think, *"Does this really work?"* Or, *"That sounds nice for you, Kerry, but you really don't know my situation. That would never work for me."* I understand how you feel. But I also understand that God doesn't give us commands without a purpose.

Consider your job. Chances are you don't feel like going to work every day, no matter how much you love what you do. But when was the last time you said to yourself, "I can't go to work tomorrow. I just don't feel like it." I doubt you've ever said anything like that. It's more likely you've told yourself, "I don't feel like going to work, but I'm going to go anyway, because it's the right thing to do, and I know there will be a big payoff in the end."

What if the same were true for love?

Consider the positive cycle you could set in motion by choosing to act in a loving way, even when you didn't feel like it.

Let's say you have a conflict with your husband. Both of you walk away from the conflict with negative feelings toward each other that lead to more negative thoughts. You might think, *"He always acts like this!"* or *"He's just being selfish."* Meanwhile, he's thinking the same thing about you. If both of you respond to your negative feelings about each other by acting in negative ways, you'll add fuel to the fire of those negative feelings, and the conflict can last a lifetime.

> If we let negative feelings lead our behavior, we only get more negative feelings.
> #abeautifullife

On the other hand, what if you choose to act in a way that's counterintuitive and counter-cultural? What if you choose to do the opposite of what you feel? Maybe he is being unreasonable and insensitive, but you choose to act loving toward him anyway (trust me, I know that's hard). Suddenly, his feelings toward you change, which changes his thoughts about you, which changes his actions. Now you're fueling the fire of positive feelings, rather than negative ones!

This kind of love is undeserved and hard to give in the moment, but like going to work when you don't feel like it, it's the right thing to do. And trust me, the benefits for your relationships are huge. You're sowing into a beautiful life!

Do you have negative feelings toward someone in your life? Do those feelings cause you to act toward that person in unloving ways? Do those unloving actions give you *more* unloving feelings, or *less?* What would it look like for you to act loving, even when you don't feel that way?

● ● ●

"It's not about doing what we feel like;
it's about doing what God says."

JOYCE MEYERS

CHAPTER ELEVEN

Love Comes Close

"'I'm telling the solemn truth: Whenever
you did one of these things
to someone overlooked or ignored, that
was me—you did it to me.'"

MATTHEW 25:40, MSG

For most of my life, I assumed Matthew 25 was a passage that instructed us how to treat the poor and give to missions. I believed it with all my heart, and made this a priority in my life. And while giving to needy people is necessary and good, what I didn't realize is that the message of this passage extends far beyond those who are poor or who don't know Jesus. The way we treat every single person we come into contact with throughout the course of our day is a reflection of how we treat Jesus.

Love doesn't just care about a problem that's distant. Love doesn't only send money to an issue that's far away. Love comes close, like Jesus came close to show God's love for humanity on earth. I don't know about you, but for me, that's convicting.

> Every personal encounter we have is an opportunity to show love.
> #abeautifullife

One day this passage came alive for me in a whole new way. As I read through this passage, just as I had a dozen other times, it suddenly occurred to me: "What I do for the *least* of these brothers" represents not only the people "out there" in the world who are hurt or broken, it represents the people who are near to me, the people God had placed in my life (discussed in Chapter 8). They have needs, too, and God wants to use me to meet them.

Because I believe Scripture is powerful, and God has the ability to illuminate Scripture for you in the same way He did for me, I want to include the entire passage here. As you read through it, consider how love comes close:

When the Son of Man comes in his glory, and all the angels with him, he will sit on his glorious throne. All the nations will be gathered before him, and he will separate the people one from another as a shepherd separates the sheep from the goats. He will put the sheep on his right and the goats on his left.

Then the King will say to those on his right, "Come, you who are blessed by my Father; take your inheritance, the kingdom prepared for you since the creation of the world. For I was hungry and you gave me something to eat, I was thirsty and you gave me something to drink, I was a stranger and you invited me in, I needed clothes and you clothed me, I was sick and you looked after me, I was in prison and you came to visit me."

Then the righteous will answer him, "Lord, when did we see you hungry and feed you, or thirsty and give you something to drink? When did we see you a stranger and invite you in, or needing clothes and clothe you? When did we see you sick or in prison and go to visit you?"

The King will reply, "Truly I tell you, whatever you did for one of the least of these brothers and sisters of mine, you did for me."

Then he will say to those on his left, "Depart from me, you who are cursed, into the eternal fire prepared for the devil and his angels. For I was hungry and you gave me nothing to eat, I was thirsty and you gave me nothing to drink, I was a stranger and you did not invite me in, I needed clothes and you did not clothe me, I was sick and in prison and you did not look after me."

They also will answer, "Lord, when did we see you hungry or thirsty or a stranger or needing clothes or sick or in prison, and did not help you?"

He will reply, "Truly I tell you, whatever you did not do for one of the least of these, you did not do for me.

Then they will go away to eternal punishment, but the righteous to eternal life."

(Matthew 25:31–46)

I don't know about you, but reading this passage, in light of the realization that every human interaction is a reflection of how I treat Jesus, challenges me. Think about the implications of this. Each time I make a meal for a friend who just had a baby, or invite a young single person to my house for Thanksgiving dinner, or stop to buy a cup of hot chocolate for the woman begging for money on the side of the road, or take time to listen to my coworker's problem, I am doing it for Jesus.

Jesus cares about giving money to charity and to missions. But He cares *just as much* how we love those closest to us.

After really understanding this passage of Scripture, I now see every personal encounter as an opportunity to clothe, feed, and comfort Jesus. Each day, I'm presented with opportunities to meet the tangible needs of people God places in my path. Each day, I'm given opportunities to move close to the people God entrusts to me. In each of these moments, I have the opportunity to demonstrate my love for Christ.

The Power of Coming Close

Coming close is about moving towards others, and inviting others to move toward you. My husband, Mike, a longtime pastor, says, "Belonging is the beginning of believing and becoming." In other words, when people feel they belong somewhere—when they feel they're part of a group and people care about them—they're able to believe in Jesus and become who God made them to be.

Most people think this happens the other way around. Most of us, perhaps without realizing it, act as if a person should *believe* in Jesus and *become* loveable before we accept them into our community. But love comes close, even to those who don't deserve it. Love invites people in. Love includes. *Belonging* is the beginning of believing and becoming.

Can you think of a time someone reached out to you, even when you didn't ask for it or feel you "deserved" it? Perhaps you were new to a city or a church and someone invited you in. Maybe you felt left out at school, and someone asked you to sit at their lunch table. How did their invitation make you feel? I'm guessing it was incredibly life-changing.

> EACH DAY, I'M PRESENTED WITH OPPORTUNITIES TO MEET THE TANGIBLE NEEDS OF PEOPLE GOD PLACES IN MY PATH.

Coming close isn't just about inviting people in, it's about focusing on the needs of others before your own. My husband and I have done a fair amount of marriage counseling over the years, and one of the most important—and most interesting—topics we cover is what happens in the bedroom after the wedding. Sex, the most powerful earthly image of intimacy and the ultimate example of "coming close," is best when both people in the relationship choose to focus on each other more than themselves.

This is completely counter-cultural and, for that reason, a little hard for most women to believe. But we've counseled enough married couples to know it's true. When a wife thinks more about her husband's wants, needs, and desires than she thinks about her own—and the husband does the same—they discover greater intimacy over time.

Anytime we grow selfish, our relationships become unhealthy.

I wonder if you feel dissatisfied, not only in your marriage, but in all your relationships. Maybe you feel as if you have many needs and none of them are being met. Perhaps you feel disconnected, unloved, or forgotten. Quite possibly, the answer to your problem might not be to have more of your needs met by others—but to meet the needs of others, instead. The answer might be to *come close.*

What if you looked at your relationships the way a farmer looks at his crops? Each day, the farmer wakes up and tends to the crops in his field. He takes great care, knowing that if he neglects the crops, he'll have nothing to eat at harvest time. He thinks carefully about what each plant needs. He waters, feeds, and cares for it. He knows that if he doesn't care for his own crops no one will. He takes personal responsibility to care for them.

This is love. Love thinks ahead. Love plans. Love visits, feeds, waters, meets needs, and waits to see growth. Who are the people in your life who need this from you? Are you coming close to them?

When we choose to come close to those who need our love, when we care for them, and meet their needs, the craziest thing happens. One of our deepest and most important needs is met as well—the need to honor Jesus. Whatever you do for those God has put in your life, you do for Him.

•   •   •

"Love is the accurate estimate and adequate supply of another person's needs."

DICK FOTH

CHAPTER TWELVE

Apathy Is the Opposite of Love

"He will answer them, 'I'm telling you the solemn truth:
Whenever you failed to do one of these
things to someone who was being
overlooked or ignored, that was me—you failed to do it to me.'"

MATTHEW 25:45, MSG

A s I continued to ponder the passage in Matthew 25 that we discussed in the previous chapter, I sat back and wondered to myself: *Why don't I do a better job of loving those around me. I see there are needs, don't I? Why haven't I reached out to meet them? I dutifully give money to charities and missions and the church. Why don't I spend more time, money, or resources to help the people in my immediate circles?*

I thought of a few different reasons. It's logistically easier to send money than it is to make a meal, for example. I'm busy and probably a little self-centered (like the rest of us). I have other things on my mind. But the biggest realization I had was that it's easier, emotionally, to help those who are far from me. I don't have to feel much compassion. It doesn't take much energy or emotion to write a check. To help someone close to me, on the other hand, is much more difficult and can get complicated.

> APATHY DOESN'T JUST KEEP US FROM HELPING OTHERS, IT KEEPS US FROM A BEAUTIFUL LIFE.

When we move close to people who are hurting or in need, it's impossible not to care. It's easy to stay angry at my husband while I remain emotionally distant from him, but when I ask him why he's hurting, and he begins to share, my anger melts away and I have compassion. It's easy to judge the woman on the side of the road for the bad decisions that led her there, but when I come close and hear her story, it's impossible not to feel compassion for the difficulties she faces.

When we come close to others, we suffer with them, the same way Jesus came close to suffer with us.

Based on the parable of the sheep and the goats in Matthew 25, I've challenged myself to come close to those around me—to overcome the obstacles of time, money, and resources, and begin to meet the needs of my community. I'm confronting my own selfishness and sense of entitlement so I can love others well.

Debunking the Hate Myth

Most of us think the opposite of love is hate, but we're wrong. Noted author and concentration camp survivor Elie Wiesel has famously stated: "The opposite of love is not hate, it's indifference." In other words, the opposite of love is *apathy*. Consider a parent who wastes money on drugs and alcohol, while their child goes hungry. Though the parent isn't doing anything to hurt the child purposefully, their neglect hurts the child a great deal. We would all agree this is unloving at best—disgraceful at worst. But the same is true for us when we see a need and have the ability to meet it, yet we choose not to.

We can't ignore the importance of this any longer. Apathy doesn't just keep us from helping others, it keeps us from a beautiful life. The good news is we have everything we need to move close to those around us, to love them. Here are some practical steps to help you move close to others.

FIRST, DETERMINE THE NEED. Most of us are so locked into our own lives—going to work, driving the kids to practice, making dinner, getting some sleep, and doing it all over again—that we don't have any idea what's going on outside our circle. In order to determine the needs around us, we need to open our eyes.

Pay attention to the people you see on a daily basis. Ask them how they're doing. Notice the looks on their faces. People might tell you they're "doing fine," but you can tell from their grimace that they're *not* doing fine. As you build a relationship with those people, offer to help in any way you can.

Offer to pray for them and *do it.* Even better, ask if you can stop and pray for them right there. If it makes them uncomfortable, respect that wish, but if not, it can be powerful to pray in the moment. Often, in prayer, the Holy Spirit gives us a supernatural picture of that person's need.

Do you see how you can't truly determine a person's need without coming close to them?

NEXT, DETERMINE HOW YOU CAN MEET THE NEED. I say "how" instead of "if" because there are many ways to meet a need. For example, sometimes the most obvious need is something expensive, complicated, or out of reach. If a friend is going through a divorce, you can't be their divorce attorney, marriage counselor, or social worker (unless you actually *are* one of those things). But you can offer a hug, a word of encouragement, or a safe place to grieve.

> Apathy keeps us from experiencing a beautiful life.
> #abeautifullife

One of the best ways to determine how you can meet a need is simply to ask. You might say, "It looks like you've had a hard week. Is there anything I can do for you?"

The closer you get to people, the more you'll know them. The more you know them, the less you'll need to ask, "What can I do?" With those you've already been loving and serving, you might be able to say, "I know your car broke down yesterday. Can I take you to work this week?" or "I know your husband is in the hospital. Can I bring you a meal so you don't have to cook?" This is what it looks like to love people up close.

FINALLY, IF YOU STRUGGLE TO COME CLOSE TO PEOPLE, CONFRONT YOUR OWN APATHY. This is the hardest task of all because at one time or another most of us feel justified in our apathy. We feel that the needs of others are overwhelming, or that we have too many needs of our own.

Instead of loving others, apathetic people feel sorry for themselves (it's an easy trap) and expect other people to feel sorry for them, too.

If this is you, I want to encourage you lovingly: confront your own apathy.

Are you loving people well? Are you coming close to others?

Don't get me wrong. We can't take on everything (even Jesus didn't end all suffering while He was on earth), and I'm not suggesting we love from a place of guilt. But when we do everything we can, with what we have, for those in need—especially those closest to us—our marriages change, our relationships thrive, the walls fall down, and we feel more alive, beautifully alive!

     ● ● ●

"We always want to be asking God what He is doing and how He wants us to work with Him."

DALLAS WILLARD

Going Deeper
PART FOUR—LOVE IS A VERB

DISCUSSION OR JOURNAL QUESTIONS

1. What's the difference between allowing our feelings to lead our responses and being obedient to God's instructions? How can allowing negative feelings to lead our behavior lead to more negative feelings? How can doing the right thing change our negative feelings?

2. Love comes close. Read Matthew 25:31–46. The author said she has begun to see every personal encounter as an opportunity to demonstrate her love for Christ. How could that mindset change the way we interact with people every day?

3. Apathy is the opposite of love. Reread Matthew 25:41–46. These are some of the most sobering words in Scripture. Jesus doesn't say, "Depart from me because you murdered or lied." He says, "Depart from me because you were apathetic; you didn't respond with love." How can we confront our apathy?

A PERSONAL CHALLENGE

Since love is so much more than an emotion, how you can demonstrate your love to those who are closest to you this week? Look at every personal encounter as an opportunity to express your love for Christ. Journal how you have loved differently this week.

Be Kind

. . .

S ome of the most incredible examples of human love are Holocaust survivors like Corrie ten Boom and missionaries like Lillian Trasher and Mother Teresa. We can all learn something about love from these influential people.

At the same time, there's a certain danger in setting such a high example of love for ourselves. Suddenly we begin to feel that giving love is out of our reach. We wonder if we have to move to a foreign country, or start a ministry to the homeless in order to be a loving person. Based on that standard, we might feel like we don't have the resources, the personality, or the know-how to be a person of great love.

Certainly, some of you who are reading this book *will* move to a foreign country or start a nonprofit or ministry. Others of you won't. Either way, in this section I want to discuss how love can be simple. You have everything you need to be hospitable, to give grace, and to serve. It doesn't take any special training. It's not reserved for those who have a certain income. Everyone can show love this way. All it takes is a humble and ready heart.

Is your heart humble and ready?

As you read through the next three chapters, think how you can demonstrate love—simply by being kind—to those in your immediate circle. Imagine ways you can use what you already have. Be creative and be thoughtful, but most of all be humble and teachable. Ask God to show you who He wants you to love.

As you put one foot in front of the other on your path toward kindness, don't be surprised if something incredible emerges. This is the road to a beautiful life.

CHAPTER THIRTEEN

Biblical Hospitality Has Nothing to Do with Martha Stewart

"Offer hospitality to one another without grumbling."

1 PETER 4:9

It's interesting to me that our key verse for this book (1 Peter 4:8) is followed with a command to be hospitable. When it comes to hospitality, I think most women have one of two interpretations. Either a woman takes on the burden of extravagant hospitality—creating elaborate environments and going to extreme lengths to cook meals and maintain a house that looks like it's from a magazine; or a woman says to herself, "that's too much work. I must not have the gift of hospitality."

There's nothing wrong with going to great lengths to make someone feel comfortable in your home—fancy foods, soft linens, perfectly made beds are wonderful—but I don't think this is what Scripture means when it says to "offer hospitality to one another." It doesn't fit with what we know about members of the early church—many of whom did *not* live in luxury. What I think it means is that we're called to open our lives and our doors to one another.

To explain what I mean by this, let me tell you a story.

I have a friend who recently traveled to Guatemala to visit a child she had sponsored there. After her trip, I asked about her time there, and her face lit up. She said, "Kerry, if I had to use one word to describe my time there, I would use this word: *hospitality.*" I asked what she meant by that, and this is what she told me:

> Honestly, I thought hospitality was a huge priority of mine. I grew up in a family who offered meals and beds to anyone who needed them, anytime, no questions asked, and I've always had a strong desire to do the same. My husband and I talk about this often, about how one of the things we most want in life is a space that would let us open our doors to friends and strangers for meals or a place to sleep.
>
> We have weekly conversations about what exactly we could do to make people feel loved and cared for in our home, and dream about a space where people would feel comfortable and safe.
>
> But it wasn't until I went to Guatemala that I realized I've been *waiting* to practice hospitality until I have a bigger house and nicer stuff. The families in Guatemala taught me what hospitality really is.

In the time we were there, several families took chickens from their yards and used them to cook meals for us. These meals weren't elaborate by my standards, but normally that type of meal would only be served at weddings or festivals. One family even offered to give us a live chicken to take home with us. (I was so disappointed we had to decline. Can you just see us carrying our chicken through customs?).

Their houses are made from mud and they have nothing but makeshift furniture, yet they eagerly invited us into their homes. I was so shocked by that. Since my husband and I are newly married, and still building our lives together, I sometimes neglect to invite people into our home, telling myself I'd rather wait until it's "ready." But the people of Guatemala weren't waiting for anything. They invited us to take a seat at their kitchen tables or on their *beds* and make ourselves comfortable.

Their laundry was swaying in the wind; it wasn't perfectly folded and put away in drawers, but they invited us anyway.

While we were there, they unabashedly breast-fed their children.

They shared openly about their struggles and needs, and invited us to share openly with them. ("How have you been married for a year and a half but you haven't had any children?") I loved the transparency they practiced, with us, and in their community.

They weren't waiting until they had "enough" to share. They simply shared. They weren't waiting for a home or a space that was conducive to inviting guests. They weren't waiting for the perfect guest room, or a beautiful L-shaped couch, or a cupboard overflowing with food in order to invite people over for dinner. They had very little to give, but they gave everything. And that made what they gave seem like so much.

I have so much to learn from them. I want to learn to give like they gave to us, without waiting until I have enough, because I'm already enough. I already have enough. I don't have to wait any longer. Being hospitable is simply about opening the door to what I already have.

When I heard my friend's story, I thought, *"Yes, exactly. Hospitality is about opening the door to what you already have."* And yet, if it really is this simple, why aren't more of us practicing true hospitality?

What Keeps Us From Offering Hospitality?

When I asked my friend what had kept her from being hospitable before her life-changing trip to Guatemala, she responded, "I think it was pride." She explained how she was afraid to invite people over to her house or into her life because she was scared of what they would think of her based on what she had or didn't have. She was afraid they would think her home was not nice enough.

"I'm afraid they'll reject me and go away," she said.

If you ask me, this is a real and common fear. And yet, it is unfounded. Chances are, when we share what we have with people, no strings attached, their response will be the same as the response my friend had to the people of Guatemala—humility, awe, and gratitude. If the response is something different (unkind words, judgment, etc.) it reflects poorly on the receiver not on the giver.

Imagine if my friend in Guatemala had reacted differently. After one of the village women had cooked some chicken soup and handed her a steaming bowl with a glowing smile on her face, what if my friend had said, "That's disgusting. I'll never eat that!"? Who would look uglier in that situation? The answer is obvious. Hospitality is always a *beautiful* thing to do.

Hospitality turns the attention *off* of self and onto the other. In the *Anne of Green Gables* books, there's a beautiful scene where Anne is invited to tea with the pastor's wife, and she worries

> HOSPITALITY IS ABOUT OPENING THE DOOR TO WHAT YOU ALREADY HAVE.

about the proper rules of etiquette. She says, "I'm so afraid I'll do something silly or forget to do something I'm supposed to do." Marilla gives her great advice. She says, "The trouble with you, Anne, is that you're thinking too much about yourself. You should think of Mrs. Allan and what would be nicest and most agreeable to her."[5]

I think if we're honest with ourselves, most of us have the same problem. We think too much about ourselves and not enough about others. What if we changed our focus? What would that do for our hospitality? What if we abandoned our pride and started thinking about others more than ourselves?

The next time you're at church, rather than wondering what would have to change for *you* to be more comfortable, look around and find someone who seems uncomfortable. Are they new? Are they by themselves? Do they seem sad or lonely? Ask yourself what you could do to make them feel at ease. Maybe you could invite them to sit with you and your family; or invite them to lunch. This is hospitality.

> Hospitality is, simply opening the door to yourself.
> #abeautifullife

I want to share 1 Peter 4:7–11 in Eugene's Peterson's *The Message*. It explains so well what Peter meant when he urged believers to "practice hospitality." Take some time to read this passage and consider how you might show hospitality in your own way.

> Love makes up for practically anything. Be quick to give a meal to the hungry, a bed to the homeless— cheerfully. Be generous with the different things God gave you, passing them around so all get in on it: if words, let it be God's words; if help, let it be God's hearty help. That way, God's bright presence will be evident in everything through Jesus, and he'll get all the credit as the One mighty in everything—encores to the end of time. Oh, yes!

Do you get the picture? Biblical hospitality has nothing to do with Martha Stewart. You don't have to be able to bake a beautiful cake or have the perfect home in order to be hospitable (thank goodness). Hospitality simply means opening the door to what you have, whether that's time, words, space, gifts, or something else entirely. Hospitality is about putting others before yourself, making them comfortable where they otherwise might not be. It's that simple, and that beautiful.

When we open the doors to what we have and who we are, all of heaven sighs and says, "Oh, yes!"

• • •

"I'm not sure exactly what heaven will be like, but I know that when we die and it comes time for God to judge us, He will not ask, 'How many good things have you done in your life?' rather He will ask, 'How much love did you put into what you did?'"

MOTHER TERESA

CHAPTER FOURTEEN

Full of Grace and Mercy

"Blessed are the merciful, for they will be shown mercy."

MATTHEW 5:7

I have a close friend named Ariel, and while I was writing this book, she shared an experience that demonstrates perfectly how grace requires us to get our hands dirty.

Ariel had known Jamie since high school. A young woman who was very gifted musically, Jamie led worship at their church. She had an incredible ability to lead a group of musicians and invite a crowd into worship. God used her talents and influence, and her popularity grew.

Eventually, Jamie received an offer to join a band. It wasn't a Christian band, but it would be a great opportunity for her career and would provide publicity for her talents. When Jamie decided to join the band, Ariel couldn't help but worry how a band environment might hurt Jamie's walk with God.

After she joined the band, Jamie soon began to make compromises in her life. Rumors spread about her poor decisions, and she became an outcast in their church community and city.

Ariel grieved over the decisions her friend was making. Since Jamie knew God's truth, Ariel couldn't understand why she would make such devastating compromises that negatively impacted so many people. The longer this went on, the more negative thoughts and feelings Ariel had about Jamie.

One day, Ariel and her husband received a call from Jamie's husband. He asked them to come over to their apartment to help them with a project.

At first, Ariel told me, the idea was disgusting. She simply didn't want to spend time around Jamie. But before she could open her mouth the Holy Spirit whispered to her, "Don't treat her that way." The words pierced Ariel's heart, and she became compassionate about Jamie's life and grew tender toward her. She felt sorry for the way others had mistreated her and rejected her.

So instead of brushing off the invitation, Ariel and her husband agreed to go help the young couple with the project.

On the drive to Jamie's apartment, Ariel's stomach was in knots. Even though she was nervous about the encounter, she believed that God could use her to offer grace and hope. A sense of calm settled over the car before they arrived.

Ariel and her husband spent time helping Jamie and her family with the project. They weren't there long, but they had showed up to lend a hand.

In the car, on the way home, Ariel turned to her husband.

"I really don't feel like we did anything."

"We didn't," her husband said. "We were just there. That was enough."

Months later, Jamie's husband texted them to say, "Thanks for being our safe place." In that moment Ariel realized why the Holy Spirit had urged them to go over to their apartment in the first place—to show God's love.

As Ariel told me this story, I thought how powerful it can be when we simply love people. This is the way Jesus treats us, isn't it? He comes to us. He comforts us. He brings food for our souls and our bodies. It's messy sometimes. We may choose to walk down some wobbly roads, but He comes to us anyway. He doesn't lecture us. He loves us and leaves the sweet fragrance of His love behind.

I think we sometimes fail to give grace like this because we want to see results more than we want to be gracious. If a friend gets trapped in sin of some kind, we want to see her give up her sinful ways *more* than we want to see her loved. And, like Ariel, we worry the friend's reputation will tarnish ours, or people will think we condone her mistakes.

> WE'RE NOT CALLED TO CONTROL ANYONE'S ACTIONS. WE'RE SIMPLY CALLED TO LOVE.

We want so badly for the friend to change that any interaction we have with her becomes about encouraging change. If she doesn't change right away, we want to give up.

But what if we left the changing to Jesus? What if we just loved? What would that look like? I think it would look like Ariel going to her friend's apartment to lend a helping hand. Although she didn't feel like she had done much, she had demonstrated love—and that's what it's all about.

We're not called to change anyone. We're not called to control anyone's actions. We're simply called to love.

Love Heals

Sometimes it's hard to believe love can be as powerful a change agent as I'm stressing here. I think most of us worry, "If I give too much grace, won't this person just go on hurting themselves and hurting others?" While I understand the fear, I think it's unwarranted.

"Love heals" is the motto of a nonprofit called Thistle Farms based in Nashville, Tennessee. Thistle Farms is a social enterprise that started because a woman named Becca Stevens wanted to help women in the area recover from drug and alcohol addictions and criminal convictions.

She had started a recovery house—The Magdalene House— but noticed that when women came out of the two-year recovery program they had a hard time reintegrating into society. With little to no work history and criminal convictions on their records, most of the women had a hard time earning an honest living to support their families. So Becca decided to help them by starting a business of her own, where she could hire them.

She called the business Thistle Farms, not because it was on a farm (it wasn't) but because the thistle is a unique flower that's incredibly resilient, can grow anywhere (usually between the cracks on the pavement), and blossoms with a beautiful, unexpected, purple flower. She considers Thistle

Farms a place where "thistles" can grow and blossom into something totally unexpected.

The women of Thistle Farms use natural herbs and plants, such as the thistle, to create all-natural paper products, body products, soaps, candles, and healing oils, which they sell online, at house parties, and in major retailers (like Whole Foods). Not only have hundreds of women been rescued from a life of drugs, prostitution, and criminal convictions, they've been given dignity, along with an opportunity to work with their hands and provide financial support for their families.

Grace is so powerful it can transform people from rough and tough weeds that grow up from the cracks of the pavement to beautiful purple flowers. This is the strength of grace— if we're willing to offer it.

> Grace is messy. In order to give it, you have to get your hands dirty. #abeautifullife

Grace in Real Life

I don't share this story so you can start your own social enterprise that rescues women from the streets and gives them a place of employment. Becca is a special person with a special anointing for that specific dream. If God has given you a calling like Becca's, by all means, go after it. But for most of us, giving grace in real life will look a little different. Each of us is called to offer God's transforming power of grace and love.

Kindness should permeate our lives—it should be obvious in our facial expressions, tone of voice, and body language. It should be a way of life. In order for this to happen, we must start with our thoughts and beliefs. Proverbs 4:23 says, "Guard your heart, for everything you do flows from it." In other words, what your heart believes, your mind will think, which will seep out of your entire being. The foundation for grace-filled actions is grace-filled thoughts.

What do your words and actions say about what's in your heart? Think of your most recent interactions with the people you care about. Consider a conversation with your husband, or your mom, or your sister. Were the words that came out of your mouth loving words? Were they kind words? Were they filled with grace?

Sometimes we act kindly to a person's face, but still have negative thoughts or feelings about that person. Do you have a problem with gossip or backbiting? Do you talk about people when they're not around? The next time you catch yourself doing that, ask yourself if you would say what you're saying if the person you're talking about were standing right in front of you.

If you sense that your words and actions might not live up to the kind of love you hope to give, don't beat yourself up. In the next chapter, I'm going to share how to give love space to grow in your life.

● ● ●

"Let your focus be on the creative and the constructive above the critical and corrective."

DR. GEORGE O. WOOD

CHAPTER FIFTEEN

Love Grows
When We Serve

"Use your freedom to serve one another in love; that's how freedom grows."

GALATIANS 5:13, MSG

For most of us, serving doesn't come naturally. In fact, I think serving those who aren't kind to us is one of the most difficult spiritual disciplines to embrace. Many years ago, God really began to deal with my perspective on this.

I was having a difficult time with a coworker. Actually, I wasn't the only one who had a hard time with this person. Most people in the office found her demanding and impossible to please. She asked for things that seemed ridiculous. She was a perfectionist who seemed, at times, like she was just trying to ruin everyone's day.

One day I submitted a report to her, and she placed it back on my desk and asked me to change the margins.

It was tempting, at first, to react to her the way everyone reacted to her: gossip about how impossible she was, ignore her ridiculous demands, and roll my eyes at her outlandish requests. But for some reason, I felt God urge me to do something different. I felt Him urge me to serve her.

So instead of ignoring her demands, I did everything I could to meet them. In fact, I tried to go above and beyond what she asked. I looked for needs that fell outside my normal responsibilities and tried to invent ways to meet those, too. Occasionally I brought her coffee, volunteered to work on projects everyone else avoided, and wrote her notes of appreciation.

> LOVE HAPPENS AS WE TURN OUR EYES OFF OF OURSELVES AND ONTO OTHERS.

As I worked to serve her, the most incredible thing happened. I grew to love her, and I think she grew to like me, too. The more kindness and service I offered, the more her tough, icy exterior melted, and eventually we became great friends.

This experience changed my mind about service and the role it plays in love. We don't serve *because* we love. We love *because* we serve. The more we serve people, the more we love them.

It's strange how this happens, but the longer I practice it the more I realize it's true. We serve babies, and we love them more every day. We serve our spouses, and our love deepens. We serve our parents or our children and we grow to love them more and more. We travel to another country and serve a group of people in need and we grow to love them. They become a part of our hearts, and we become part of theirs.

In this sense, love happens to us as we work, as we serve, as we clear our hearts of negative thoughts and replace them with kind, gracious ones. Love happens as we turn our eyes off of ourselves and onto others. Love happens as we draw close to those around us. How do I know? Because love is happening to me this way, and the more I lean into it, the more beautiful my love grows.

Grow in Love

We frequently use the phrase "fall in love," but I don't think that accurately describes the process of love. I think it's more like we "grow in love." By this I mean that our devotion to serve others, to give ourselves for them, is what causes our love to grow for them.

So, if you feel that love is lacking in your life, I recommend you start by serving. Chances are, if you're like most women I meet, you already serve in many areas of life, but you might not have the right mindset about it. Perhaps you drive your kids to soccer practice and prepare dinner for your spouse or family every night. Perhaps you serve women in your church by meeting with them to talk about life or buy them coffee.

Consider how your job might be an act of service. Just because you get paid doesn't mean you aren't serving. Are you changing diapers for a job? Teaching? Serving hamburgers at a local restaurant? Whatever you're doing, consider even the most mundane daily task—delivering an extra side of ranch to a table or being kind to someone who is rude to you—an act of worship.

Consider how you might bring the presence of Christ into your every activity.

Most of us don't need to feel guilty that we're not serving enough. We simply need to recognize how *much* we're already serving. We need to see every act of service as an act of worship, and treat it as such. Rather than resenting acts of service or dreading them, we can offer them up as a sacrifice—as love to God and love to others. When we do this, our love will inevitably grow.

> The more we serve people, the more we grow to love them.
> #abeautifullife

Is there someone you find hard to love? I challenge you to serve that person. I encourage you to find out what they need and offer it to them. Pray for them. I would be surprised if you were able to maintain your negative feelings toward them. When you serve someone—genuinely serve them—it's hard to feel anything but compassion, love, and empathy.

What if you were willing to see every act of service as an act of worship? What steps can you take to turn the mundane into the beautiful?

• • •

"We ought not to be weary of doing the little things for God, who regards not the greatness of the work, but the love with which it is performed."

BROTHER LAWRENCE

Going Deeper
PART FIVE—BE KIND

DISCUSSION OR JOURNAL QUESTIONS

1. Biblical hospitality has nothing to do with Martha Stewart. Aren't you thankful for that? Most of us will never measure up to our idea of being the perfect hostess. Hospitality is thinking more about others and making them comfortable. How does this definition change your idea of hospitality?

2. We are called to be full of grace and mercy. Knowing that our thoughts direct our behavior, consider what could change if you practiced grace-filled thoughts about other people. How can you discipline your mind to be full of mercy rather than judgment and criticism?

3. Love grows when we serve. Discuss the love we have for babies who are completely dependent upon us for every need. How is that an example of love growing as we serve? Discuss a time when your perspective of someone changed when you decided to serve them rather than demand something from them. How can every act of service for people become an act of worship and an expression of our love for God?

A PERSONAL CHALLENGE

George O. Wood said, "Let your focus be on the creative and the constructive above the critical and corrective." This week, discipline your thoughts to be on the creative and the constructive. Refuse to allow critical, corrective thoughts to linger. Watch how this transforms your responses to others. Take time to journal the impact of simply shifting your focus.

PART SIX

Manage Conflicts Well

• • •

I want to challenge your thinking: conflicts are not bad. In fact, conflicts are a normal, healthy part of life, growth, and change. Conflict in life is inevitable and necessary, but you can learn to manage it well. This is one key to experiencing and growing a beautiful life.

In this section, I'd like to explore how to manage conflicts well. Sometimes this means taming the conflict, sometimes it means working hard to achieve resolution, and it always requires guarding our responses. Conflict can get ugly; it can be destructive, and ultimately, you can't control how others will respond in conflict. But in this section of the book we'll help you know when to overlook an offense, how to keep the conflict from getting out of hand, and how to watch your own responses.

No one enjoys conflict. (It isn't fun writing about it either.) But it's important for us to understand what we bring to the conflict so we can begin to change the conflicts in our lives. When you learn how to manage conflict well, your relationships will become deeper and more rewarding.

I want to offer you some strategies that have helped me deal with conflict, so you don't feel as though you come to these moments empty-handed. I hope they help you, too.

CHAPTER SIXTEEN

Know When to Overlook an Offense

"A person's wisdom yields patience; it is to one's glory to overlook an offense."

PROVERBS 19:11

T here was a time when I wasn't good at managing conflict. When something happened that upset me, I wouldn't bring it up (for fear of not sounding nice), but I also wouldn't curb my negative thoughts toward the person who had caused the hurt. As a result, I carried a heavy burden of offenses I wasn't sure how to put down.

Let me share a story. A few years ago, my husband, Mike, went to the store to pick up a few things, and while he was there he ran into a friend of ours, Hilary. He asked Hilary how she was doing, and she told him she was okay but that her mother had just died. He gave his condolences, although there wasn't much he could do right there in the grocery store. He assured her he would relay the information to me when he returned home.

But when he walked in the front door, he was on the phone, and by the time he hung up, the information about Hilary's mom slipped his mind.

For the next few weeks, it seemed as if Hilary ignored me completely. I was confused. Had I done something to offend her? Was she okay? Three weeks after the fact, I bumped into her at a church function.

"Hilary!" I said. "How have you been?"

She glared at me. "I can't believe you," she said. "You didn't even send me a sympathy card! How could you be so insensitive! I lost my mother, and you haven't even acknowledged my loss!"

I must have looked confused.

"I told your husband that my mother died," she said.

My heart sank. "Oh my goodness, I didn't realize . . . " I trailed off.

For thirty minutes I worked to convince her that Mike had forgotten to tell me about her mother, but she wouldn't believe me. She was certain he would never forget to relay a message like that, and that I was simply uncaring. At first, I was struck by how difficult it was to get her to let go of her offense, but somewhere in the middle of our conversation I started to feel offended!

Trust me, I know that laying down an offense is easier said than done, but it also can be easier than it seems. As Hilary and I chose to lay down our offenses with each other, I realized that Ken Sande is right. He says in his book *The Peacemaker*, "Overlooking an offense is not a passive process." It's quite different than brooding over the event—it's deliberately deciding not to talk about it, dwell on it, or let it grow into resentment.

This means we refuse to rehearse the situation in our thoughts, talk about the issue with others, or treat the individual differently. In other words, we let it go![6]

Trust me, I know this is hard. When it came to the situation with Hilary, I had to remind myself on several occasions not to share the story with other people, not to think differently about Hilary, and not to go over the events again and again in my mind.

There are times in conflict when we choose to confront an offense, rather than overlook it (we'll talk more about that later in this section), but in this case, Hilary and I decided together to let our offenses go.

> WHEN YOU INTENTIONALLY CHOOSE TO LET AN OFFENSE GO, YOU GIVE AND RECEIVE THE GIFT OF FREEDOM.

When you intentionally choose to let an offense go, you give and receive the gift of freedom. You take a huge weight off of your shoulders, and you give yourself the opportunity to be kind and gracious toward others. As I discussed in Chapter 14, your countenance will change. You'll radiate love, kindness, and beauty from your entire being.

You literally become *more beautiful* when you choose to live a beautiful life. You make everything around you more beautiful, too.

When to Overlook an Offense

There are times when it isn't healthy to overlook an offense. Consider a conflict you faced recently. Did someone lie to you, hurt your feelings, or ignore you? Are you wondering if it was purposeful? Are you having a hard time forgetting about it? If you ignore an offense that needs to be confronted, it will make it worse. So how do you know when to confront and when to let go?

> Most of us carry offenses that are weighing us down. Choose to lay them aside, and step into a beautiful life.
> #abeautifullife

I'll talk more about *how* to confront a conflict in the next chapter, but for right now, I'd like to walk you through a few questions I always ask myself about a conflict to help me know if I should confront or overlook the offense. Answer these questions about your specific conflict on a scale from 1–10 (1 being the lowest, 10 being the highest). Be prayerful as you go through this exercise, asking God to show you the honest way to respond.

At the end, when your score is totaled, I'll help you look at your number as a way to determine whether you should confront or overlook an offense.

HOW SIGNIFICANT IS THIS PERSON IN MY LIFE? Consider the relationship you have with this person. Are they someone you encounter on a daily basis? What is the depth of your relationship with them? How important is the relationship to you? Do you want to keep it growing and thriving? For example, a family member, or a coworker who interacts with you regularly, would receive a high score on this question. A barista you'll never see again would receive a low one.

HOW SAFE DO I FEEL WITH THIS PERSON? Some people in your life just don't feel safe. Maybe they lash out at you in anger, or they have power over an area of your life that is delicate. A boss, for example, who could fire you for speaking up about a conflict, might not be very safe. A coworker who constantly loses her temper with people would receive a low score on this question. A close friend who demonstrates emotional maturity when you share your feelings with her is an example of someone who is very safe.

WILL THIS OFFENSE HINDER OUR RELATIONSHIP? If you were to let this offense go, would it hinder the relationship? If there is dishonesty, for example, will it make it harder for you to work closely with this person, or to trust them the next time you have something personal to share? This is an offense that hinders the relationship. On the other hand, if a friend forgets to call on your birthday, this is much easier to overlook.

WHAT IS THE SIZE OF THIS OFFENSE? Some offenses are small, like grapes. Others are big, like watermelons. The impact of a grape is much different than the impact of a watermelon. Minor offenses—like disagreeing with your opinion, forgetting to call on your birthday, or making an off-the-cuff rude comment— can easily be overlooked. A small offense would have a low score. Bigger offenses, like lies or betrayal, should have a high score.

ARE THERE EXTENUATING CIRCUMSTANCES THAT CAUSED THE OFFENSE? Ask yourself: Is this a repeated offense, or repeated behavior, or are there extenuating circumstances? Is the person experiencing grief? Are they overly stressed or exhausted? If a friend was short with you but has never acted that way before, chances are she was just busy or distracted. If a coworker is up all night with a sick baby, you can forgive her short temper the next day. If the behavior is repeated, or habitual, it is more likely you'll have to confront to find resolution.

Take a look at the numbers you wrote down and tally up your final score. If the number is from 31–50, it may be good for you to confront your offense. (I'll share some tools to confront an offense in the next chapter). If the score you tallied is from 1–30, prayerfully consider letting go of the offense. And remember it isn't passive! This means you don't brood over the offense, go over the offense in your mind, or talk about it with anyone else.

This is hard, I know. I've walked myself through this process a dozen times, and although it gets easier, it's never easy. But I also live so much lighter and freer these days because I'm not carrying the heavy baggage of offenses.

I don't know where you are as you read these words, but I wonder if you feel heavy with the weight of injustices you've experienced. I wonder if you feel as though you've been collecting offenses for a long time, and the frustration, anger, bitterness, and downright ugliness are overwhelming. If that's the case, take this opportunity to *lay down* the offenses that need to be abandoned.

Do you need to stop rehearsing old circumstances? Do you need to stop sharing them with other people?

I promise you won't regret laying down the heavy weight of offense. You'll never feel lighter or freer. You'll never feel more satisfied. You'll never feel closer to a beautiful life.

●   ●   ●

"It would be impossible to love God without loving others; impossible to love others unless we were grounded in a healthy self-respect; and, maybe, impossible to truly love at all in a totally secular way, without participating in the holy."

KATHLEEN NORRIS

CHAPTER SEVENTEEN

Don't Let Conflicts Get Out of Hand

*"Strive for full restoration, encourage one
another, be of one mind, live in peace.
And the God of love and peace will be with you."*

2 CORINTHIANS 13:11

S ometimes, it's best to overlook an offense. Other times, if we let conflicts go unresolved, they get out of hand, and we end up with a worse mess than need be. As I mentioned in the last chapter, when an offense is simply a personal issue, it can be overlooked in love. But when the offense might impact the long-term health and vitality of a relationship, it's good to seek resolution.

If we let the world teach us how to respond to conflict, we'll see tactics like avoidance, manipulation, and control. (I'm sure you have no idea what this looks like, but I've done my share of each.) But these selfish strategies clash with God's way of resolving conflict, which is described in Scripture.

A healthy (and biblical) way of resolving conflict always looks toward a hopeful *future* for a relationship, rather than an attempt to rehash the past. In this chapter, I want to give you a picture of what that looks like, including practical tools to help you implement this in your relationships.

The Growth of Conflicts

Have you ever noticed how quickly a conflict can get out of hand? One minute, there's simply tension between you and a friend, and before you know it (it could be thirty minutes or three weeks), the relationship seems damaged beyond repair. The sooner we address conflict and tension, the more likely it will be resolved.

> THE SOONER WE ADDRESS CONFLICT AND TENSION, THE MORE LIKELY IT WILL BE RESOLVED.

Norman Shawchuck, in his book *How to Manage Conflict in the Church, Understanding and Managing Conflict,* writes about the Conflict Cycle.[7] I've found this helps me understand the growth of conflicts, so I can resolve them early, without much drama.

If you tend to have a lot of conflict in your life, and you aren't sure how to deal with it, or if you're involved in a specific conflict right now that you aren't sure how to solve, I hope this cycle helps you pinpoint what stage you're in and ultimately leads you to resolution. The conflict cycle goes like this:

TENSION. Conflict always begins with tension. When you get that tight feeling in your gut, the awkward feeling when someone says something hurtful or the sinking feeling when you sense you're being ignored or pushed aside—pay attention to that feeling. Many people ignore conflict at this stage. (I know I have.) But it's always easier to confront or overlook an offense at this early stage in the cycle.

CONFUSION. If you let conflict with another person go beyond tension, you lose the sense of how to interact appropriately with each other. If you're in conflict with a friend, for example, the things that used to be comfortable between the two of you no longer feel comfortable. You begin to "interpret" her actions through the lens of the offense. It becomes difficult to think about her in a positive way, or to avoid talking about the issue with others.

COLLECTING OFFENSES. As the confusion grows, your mind automatically starts to fill in the things it doesn't understand by drawing conclusions that may be unfair or unfounded. For example, when a friend doesn't return your phone call, if you allow yourself to get to this late stage of the cycle, you might begin to perceive all her other actions or responses to you as a slight or "blow-off." You begin collecting offenses, like artifacts. You lose sight of the original issue. Anger, bitterness, and revenge settle in your heart.

HEALTHY CONFRONTATION OR ATTACK. Early in the conflict cycle, we can choose to have a healthy confrontation. With this tactic we make the necessary adjustments in our relationship and grow through the conflict. But when conflict goes unmanaged long enough, it escalates to attack. This is how you know that overlooking an offense is not the same as brushing it under the rug. When you overlook an offense, forgiveness follows. When you brush a conflict under the rug, it grows and escalates and eventually turns into a dangerous or unhealthy confrontation. At this stage, we can sever relationships and lose connection with people we love.

> Whether we choose to confront conflict or overlook an offense, the goal is always for restoration, hope, and a preferred future.
> #abeautifullife

GIVING UP. In this stage, those in conflict make necessary adjustments to end the confrontation and protect themselves. Although this might make us feel better in the short run, it is incredibly damaging to our hearts and spirits in the long run. Not only do we lose connection with people we care about, but we make concessions that hurt us and can ultimately sacrifice our character.

It *Is* Possible to Resolve Conflicts!

If you're tracking with me this far, I'm sure you must be wondering: *Okay, that sounds nice, but how should I confront a conflict that won't make it worse?* I'm glad you asked. That's exactly what I'd like to discuss now.

Thankfully, Matthew 18 lays out a great process for tackling conflict. I have to be honest for a minute, though. While the process spelled out in Scripture is extremely effective, it doesn't always come naturally. As women, our frequent response to conflict is to ignore our negative feelings until we can't stand them any longer, or to talk about the problem with everyone but the person involved in the conflict. I think we hope to find affirmation or comfort from somebody who will see things our way.

I understand this temptation. I've faced it and dealt with it myself. But this is never the best way to deal with conflict.

Ultimately, facing conflict head on—going straight to the source, speaking kindly and directly, and pointing toward the hope of the future—is an extremely effective and life-giving way to deal with conflict. I know it isn't comfortable to confront conflict, but if you hope to build a beautiful life—one free of strife, bitterness, and shame—this is a necessary step in that process.

So what does Matthew 18 teach us about managing conflict? Let's start by looking at the Scripture itself. The following is Matthew 18:15–17 in *The Message*. I like the simplicity of this version.

> If a fellow believer hurts you, go and tell him—work it out between the two of you. If he listens, you've made a friend. If he won't listen, take one or two others along so that the presence of witnesses will keep things honest, and try again. If he still won't listen, tell the church. If he won't listen to the church, you'll have to start over from scratch, confront him with the need for repentance, and offer again God's forgiving love.

Notice the first principle in conflict resolution is to keep the conflict as small as possible for as long as possible. We should only expand the number of people involved in the conflict as it becomes necessary to bring about repentance and reconciliation. With this goal in mind, here is the order of the expanding circle.

ONE-ON-ONE. Conflict resolution should always start with a one-on-one conversation. Never talk about it with others before you have a personal conversation with the individual(s) involved. This is the opposite of what we usually feel like doing. ("I'm just venting," we say, or "I wanted to make sure I wasn't crazy.") But when we pull others into the conflict who aren't a part of it, we're asking them to exercise grace they haven't been given. The grace for the situation rests with those who are directly involved with the conflict.

This is perhaps the most important aspect of conflict resolution, and the most difficult one to avoid, so I'm going to press this issue even further. Triangulation (when we have a problem with one person, but we talk about it with someone else) is *always* wrong, no matter what. Don't get caught in the trap of bringing a third party into your conflict before its time. These conversations only separate people from one another. We sin against others when we talk about them behind their backs.

When you confront, here are a few things to keep in mind:

- Ask questions and listen carefully to understand the situation.

- Validate the other person's feelings ("I hear you saying that you're really angry. If you thought I was ignoring you, I can see how you would feel that way.")
- Always assume there are offenses on both sides. Adopt the "plank in your own eye" mentality, and always consider how you contributed to the problem.
- Work for solutions together that solve the problem for everyone involved.

The only motive to confront should be to restore the relationship and make it better. We may be tempted to confront to point out someone's faults or to validate our negative feelings, but these are wrong motives. You don't need to seek justice for yourself. God will be your defender.

BRING A FRIEND. If the conflict is not resolved with a one-on-one conversation, ask a mature, emotionally healthy peer to be a part of the next conversation. The goal is always redemption and restoration, not to gang up on someone or to point out their faults. In fact, when you ask a friend to come with you, it might be good to communicate it like this: "We weren't able to solve our conflict on our own. Would you be willing to mediate our next conversation?"

Language like this prevents taking sides, and that's not what we really need. Instead, our goal is resolution. In this way, God gives grace to the peer who is now a participant in the conflict resolution.

WHAT DOES IT LOOK LIKE TO CALL IN LEADERSHIP? We need to be careful not to misunderstand this step. It doesn't mean you call your senior pastor to help you work out a conflict with someone in your Bible study. Instead, seek out a leader you are both accountable to. Remember, the goal is to keep the conflict as small as possible, as long as possible.

Adding leadership into the resolution process should only happen after the first two steps have failed to bring resolution. Again, it's tempting to move right to this stage of conflict resolution, but moving too quickly can do more harm than good. Remember, the goal is always redemption and restoration—never to prove your point or to "win" the conflict. If you're tempted to run to leadership before you've taken the first two steps, check your heart and motives in solving this conflict.

If you're in conflict with someone who doesn't want to find resolution, you may have to adjust the boundaries with this person or end the relationship. Resolution always requires that both parties be willing to resolve the conflict. If the conflict comes to this end, refer back to the previous section about overlooking an offense. Refuse to rehearse the situation or talk about the other person in a negative way. Continue to treat the person with respect, even from a distance.

●   ●   ●

"In conflict, when we point toward the past, we bring shame. When we point toward the future, we bring hope."

DARRELL VESTERFELT

CHAPTER EIGHTEEN

Watch Your Responses

"Make a clean break with all cutting, backbiting, profane talk.
Be gentle with one another, sensitive.
Forgive one another as quickly
and thoroughly as God in Christ forgave you"

EPHESIANS 4:31–32, MSG

When my oldest son, Tyler, was young, there was a season of his adolescence when he started to get really mouthy. If you have teenagers, maybe you can relate. Of course, as his mother, I wasn't sure how to respond at first. I was shocked by this change in his temperament. He wasn't the boy I had known for so many years, and on top of all that, his responses hurt my feelings. When he said something really ugly to me—I found myself saying something ugly right back.

At the time, it felt like the only way to respond. I didn't see how I had another choice. But later, I would look back at the situation and ask myself, "Who *was* the woman talking ugly to that boy?"

One morning, after a particularly painful confrontation with Tyler, I felt the Holy Spirit gently remind me to respond to him with humility, love, and peace. The minute I felt the correction, I knew it was right. But how would I find the strength to change my responses in the heat of the moment—when Tyler's words were so hurtful, and when my flesh seemed to take over?

> The responses you choose in conflict can either result in more conflict or lead you to a beautiful life.
> #abeautifullife

That afternoon, I read Galatians 5 from start to finish. The chapter is all about finding freedom by relying on Christ, and it warns Christians not to rely on the law, which will make them slaves once again. The only way to experience true freedom is to rely on the power of the Holy Spirit. Paul goes on to say:

> You, my brothers and sisters, were called to be free. But do not use your freedom to indulge the flesh; rather, serve one another humbly in love. For the entire law is fulfilled in keeping this one command: "Love your neighbor as yourself." If you bite and devour each other, watch out or you will be destroyed by each other.
>
> So I say, walk by the Spirit, and you will not gratify the desires of the flesh. For the flesh desires what is contrary to the Spirit, and the Spirit what is contrary to the flesh. They are in conflict with each other, so

that you are not to do whatever you want. But if you are led by the Spirit, you are not under the law.

The acts of the flesh are obvious: sexual immorality, impurity and debauchery; idolatry and witchcraft; hatred, discord, jealousy, fits of rage, selfish ambition, dissensions, factions and envy; drunkenness, orgies, and the like. I warn you, as I did before, that those who live like this will not inherit the kingdom of God. But the fruit of the Spirit is love, joy, peace, forbearance, kindness, goodness, faithfulness, gentleness and self-control. Against such things there is no law. Those who belong to Christ Jesus have crucified the flesh with its passions and desires. Since we live by the Spirit, let us keep in step with the Spirit. Let us not become conceited, provoking and envying each other. (Galatians 5:13–26)

Several things jumped off the page at me. First, I was struck by what happens when we "bite and devour" each other—Paul says we will be destroyed. I was convicted by these words because it was precisely what I saw happening with Tyler and myself. This was the last thing I wanted to take place in my family. I wanted my house to be a place of love and peace.

As a mother, I wanted nothing more than to build my family *up*. Destroying them was my worst nightmare.

Second, I noticed how Paul reminds us not to use our freedom to indulge in the flesh, but rather to "serve one another humbly, in love." *What a beautiful picture,* I thought to myself— *using my freedom in Christ to serve my son, Tyler, humbly in love.*

I'm free to respond to him however I choose. But how beautiful would it be if I used that freedom to give him grace? What might my son learn from that? What might I learn?

Third, I noticed how Paul urges believers to walk by the Spirit to avoid gratifying desires of the flesh. I knew my angry, bitter responses to Tyler were desires of the flesh; and that if I chose to walk by the Spirit, I would find the power to respond in loving ways. What I had to do was submit myself to the Spirit completely, asking continually for assurance and guidance.

Finally, the most important thing I noticed was verse 14: "For the entire law is fulfilled in this command: Love your neighbor as yourself." I was so impressed by that. Even if all other things fell away, the most important thing I could do in the whole world was to love my son. Love is the most important commandment. When I take that to heart, it should rearrange my priorities.

Feeling challenged by my time in the Word, I asked God to help me recognize that my most natural response might be wrong. The next time Tyler snapped at me, I opened my mouth to respond, and an amazing thing happened: beautiful words came out. They weren't my words. They were God's words. They were peaceful and gentle. They were loving. And when the words came out of my mouth, I turned to my son, and

THE FRUIT OF THE SPIRIT IS THE OPPOSITE OF OUR SINFUL NATURE AND IS OTHERS FOCUSED.

watched his countenance change. It turns out, when I invited the Spirit into our interaction, it changed both of us. Ultimately, God has given us a wonderful relationship of love and mutual respect.

All of a sudden, when I relied on the Holy Spirit to guide my responses in conflict, I had the opportunity to be with my son again, to influence him. I was able to step outside of myself to see that the way my son was treating me was more about him than it was about me. Then, I was able to see how I could care for him. And when I could love him as Christ has loved me—unconditionally, unfailingly, without prerequisite or requirement—it was beautiful. And I believe it was so much more pleasing to God.

How to Respond to Conflict

As Jim Van Yperen, author of *Making Peace* says, "typically our first response is wrong."[8] The most natural reactions—like mine to Tyler—are self-focused retorts of the flesh. But we don't have to allow our self-centeredness to control our reactions. The fruit of the Spirit is the opposite of our sinful nature and is *others* focused.

The fruit of the Spirit is evidenced by "love, joy, peace, forbearance, kindness, goodness, faithfulness, gentleness and self-control" (Galatians 5:22–23). So an easy way to know whether your responses are led by the Spirit or led by the flesh is to ask yourself: How do my responses look when I compare them to the fruit of the Spirit?

Since the radical transformation I experienced in my relationship with Tyler, I've taken a special interest in positive conflict resolution. I truly believe this is one of the most important things we can learn as believers. A failure to resolve conflicts well won't just impact our relationships with one another—it will impact our relationship with God as well. We can't be in conflict with another friend, coworker, or family member and *not* feel the tension in our relationship with Him.

If this is true, and conflicts are a natural, normal part of life, then we better get good at solving them. Here are some practical ideas (and review) for how to respond to conflict in a healthy, effective, Christlike way:

- Seek to know and love the other person.
- Pray to have the other person's best interests in mind.
- Don't make assumptions. Ask questions, and listen carefully to understand.
- Know when to overlook an offense and do it well.
- Pray, pray, pray.
- Look honestly at how you might be contributing to the conflict.
- Own your contribution to the conflict.
- Ask for forgiveness and generously forgive.
- Don't be defensive. Always allow God to be your defender.
- Refuse to point out the faults of others, dwell on them, or talk about them with anyone.
- Keep the conflict about the issue—don't attack the person.
- Restore gently.
- Confine the conflict to the fewest number of people possible.
- Always, always, always seek resolution and redemption (not revenge).

It's not easy to respond to conflicts well, but it is possible. With the help of the Holy Spirit, and a willing attitude, God can reshape our responses to reflect His grace and lead us to a beautiful life.

•   •   •

"True friends will always push you towards the great possibilities of your future; false friends will always chain you to the mistakes in your past."

SETH BROWN

Going Deeper
PART SIX—MANAGE CONFLICTS WELL

DISCUSSION OR JOURNAL QUESTIONS

1. We must know when to overlook an offense. Read Proverbs
   19:11. What is the outcome of pointing out every offense?
   Discuss ways to actively overlook an offense—stop brooding
   over the event, stop talking about the offense to others, and
   don't allow it to grow into resentment. Read through the
   conflict cycle on pages 125–126, and discuss the benefit of
   recognizing the tension early.

2. Don't let conflicts get out of hand. Read Matthew 18:15–17.
   Discuss the biblical outline for confronting conflict. (Use the
   material in this book to guide your discussion.) Why should
   we either overlook the offense or confront as soon as possible?

3. Watch how you respond to a conflict. How do you recognize
   inappropriate responses in conflict? How can you respond
   appropriately in conflict? (Use the material in this book to
   guide your discussion.)

A PERSONAL CHALLENGE

Darrell Vesterfelt said, "In conflict, when we point toward the
past, we bring shame. When we point toward the future, we
bring hope." Consider how you engage conflict. Do you want
to point out faults and make sure the other person knows how

they have been wrong? Simply pointing out faults is always the wrong motivation. Restoration and the hope of a better future should always guide our conversations in times of conflict. How could you engage a current conflict in a more positive way?

PART SEVEN

Forgive and You Will Be Forgiven

· · ·

Forgiveness isn't easy, but it's necessary. In fact, it might be one of the most challenging *and* important aspects of the Christian life. Matthew 6:14 says, "If you forgive other people when they sin against you, your heavenly Father will also forgive you." Our willingness to forgive is connected to God's willingness to forgive us. That's such a big deal!

And yet forgiveness can be extremely challenging. It takes a willingness to be humble, to admit our deepest hurts, and to look honestly at ourselves. What I hope to do in the following three chapters is help you to see just how beautiful the work of forgiveness can be in your life, and in those around you.

Maybe you've been holding onto small grievances. Perhaps huge injustices are looming over your head. Whether you aren't sure how to forgive, you're skeptical it even matters, or you're convinced forgiveness is impossible—I'm excited for you to read the stories that follow.

I hope you'll find yourself in them. I pray they'll help you find room for forgiveness and help you discover a beautiful life.

CHAPTER NINETEEN

Why God Wants Us to Forgive

*"In prayer, there is a connection between
what God does and what you do.
You can't get forgiveness from God, for
instance, without also forgiving others.
If you refuse to do your part, you cut
yourself off from God's part."*

MATTHEW 6:14–15, MSG

While I was writing this book, a close friend of mine encountered a conflict with her family that was extremely difficult. Her name is Natasha, and her family owns a restaurant. For decades, the entire family had worked together to keep the business running. Some waited tables, some cooked food, some managed the finances, and some cleaned the restaurant on the weekends. But no matter what the role, if you were part of the family, you were part of the business.

The problem was, working so closely together created incredible strife. I'm sure if you've ever worked with your family, you know how much work it is to maintain peace and healthy relationships.

As Natasha shared the situation with me, she was careful not to reveal too much. She didn't want her words to be construed as gossip or slander. But she needed to communicate the pain she felt. She didn't have to say much. I could see the hurt in her eyes.

THE CHOICE TO FORGIVE IS A STEP TO HEALING AND GRACE.

Natasha shared how this family conflict was impacting every aspect of her life. (Haven't we all felt this way?) She struggled to go to church or pray. She explained how every time she did, all she could think about was the tension with her family. At one point, she admitted, she actually thought to herself: *Great, this conflict with my family is even ruining my relationship with God!*

But as she continued to share with me, she explained how God was healing her heart.

"I'm starting to see what Scripture means when it says our relationship with others is connected to our relationship with God," Natasha explained. "It isn't the conflict that's getting in the way of my relationship with God. It's my lack of forgiveness— which means I have the choice to lay it down."

Over the past few months, I've watched Natasha take small, brave steps of obedience to forgive the offenses of her family. And something amazing has happened. Not only does she seem happier and more peaceful, I see her relationship with God growing. She is sure of herself, and the dreams God has put on her heart. She is a strong woman of character.

Natasha has always been beautiful, but I've seen an amazing thing happen as she surrenders this burden to Christ. She is stepping into a hopeful future, a beautiful life.

Finding Forgiveness When It Seems Impossible

Each day brings multiple opportunities to practice forgiveness. Some of the hurts are small—perhaps someone cuts in front of us in line at the bank. Others are deep and painful—like a cheating spouse or a parent who says, "I don't love you." No matter the offense, each opportunity to forgive is an opportunity to step closer to, or farther away from, Jesus.

Forgiveness is never easy. Even if the offense is small, the pain is real. And when it comes to bigger, unthinkable offenses, forgiveness gets even more challenging. We have to forgive, even when the one who offended us isn't sorry, hasn't repented, or isn't willing to change.

Regardless of the details and circumstances, forgiveness is necessary, because a decision to avoid forgiveness is a choice to walk toward even more pain. The choice to forgive is a step to healing and grace. The decision to forgive,

If you don't forgive others, God can't forgive you. #abeautifullife

while never easy, is easiest when it's made early (remember the conflict cycle). This is contrary to popular understanding, but the quicker you forgive, the easier it will be.

When you choose to hold onto that offense and allow it to grow, you experience stress, which negatively impacts your health. The longer you refuse to forgive—the more damage is done and the more likely you will see negative effects. The bitterness that results when you refuse to forgive can destroy you—physically and spiritually.

This runs parallel to Scripture, which warns us to avoid a root of bitterness because it can "cause trouble and defile many" (Hebrews 12:15).

Are you thinking about someone you haven't forgiven? Maybe the offense happened recently. Maybe it happened years ago. Perhaps you get the sense that holding on to the offense, choosing not to forgive, is hurting you spiritually, mentally, emotionally, and physically. But maybe you feel like letting go is not an option.

I hope Natasha's story encourages you. I hope you can take to heart the insight she found in her circumstance. I hope you won't wait any longer to forgive. I hope you'll find the healing, freedom, and peace that come when you offer forgiveness.

● ● ●

"To be a Christian means to excuse the inexcusable because God has forgiven the inexcusable in you."

C. S. LEWIS

CHAPTER TWENTY

Forgiveness Is
Not a Feeling

"Make allowance for each other's faults, and
forgive anyone who offends you.
Remember, the Lord forgave you, so you must forgive others."

COLOSSIANS 3:13, NLT

When I first met Chantel, I was drawn to her instantly. Do you have friends like that? You meet them and right away you like them. As our relationship grew, I learned why she is such a strong, beautiful woman—she has offered unimaginable forgiveness.

As a young girl, Chantel was sexually abused by her grandfather. When she was in her twenties she started to recognize the negative impact of those events on her life. She also learned that he had taken advantage of each of her sisters. This impacted her ability to trust men in general, to trust her husband, and even to trust God. So she began to see a Christian counselor to help her find some resolution to her pain and anger.

She was with the counselor for a year and felt like she had made some progress, but by the end of the counseling, all she could feel for her grandfather was apathy. The anger and pain was mostly gone, but in their place was a sense that the hurt didn't matter. He didn't matter.

Several years later, when their two sons had grown into young boys, Chantel and her husband decided to remodel their home. Chantel called her dad, who was a contractor, and he agreed to help. He asked to bring his father (Chantel's grandfather) to help as well.

Chantel's initial response was, "No way! He can't come to my house!" But she was in a difficult position. Since her father didn't know about the abuse, and she had already asked him to help with the remodel—there didn't seem to be a polite way to explain why she didn't want her grandfather to come.

So she conceded. "Okay, he can come," she told her husband, "but the boys will never be left alone with him, and I don't want to be around him. We'll just leave the house and let you guys do the remodel together." She had a list of rules she wanted the family to follow. She didn't want to take a picture with him, didn't want to hug him or touch him, and barely wanted to speak to him. It was as if all the negative feelings she'd held at bay for so long came flooding back in that instant.

Chantel prayed and prayed in anticipation of the day her grandfather would come. She begged God to give her what she needed to be in the same room with him, let alone to have him at her house for several days. When the day came for Chantel's grandfather and father to come to the house, she and her husband stood at the door.

"Are you ready?" her husband asked.

"No!" Chantel felt like screaming. Yet when the door swung open, and she saw her father and grandfather standing there, she felt an incredible rush of love come over her. It was as if, although her heart said, "no," her spirit said, "yes."

Chantel shared with me how she prayed non-stop through the entire visit. "God, please help me," she would say. "Give me what I need to make it through this." And, like the faithful Father He is, God did provide. She didn't ask for love. She didn't even want love. But she asked God to give her what she needed, and He gave her love. That moment, Chantel was

Forgiveness is the most freeing thing on the planet. #abeautifullife

not only able to see her grandfather for who he was, in spite of his brokenness, she also recognized the many ways he was a gift to her family.

The family maintained the boundaries they had originally agreed upon. He was never left alone with her kids, but he told the boys stories, made them laugh, and worked diligently to complete the remodel.

At one point during the weekend, Chantel's husband whispered to her, "You're doing great!"

Chantel whispered back, "It's not me!"

From that weekend on, the love Chantel felt for her grandfather never left her. In fact, it only grew. She made it a point to call and check on him, to see how he was feeling. She and her sisters prayed for him fervently, asking God to convict his heart so he would come to know Jesus.

When her grandfather was nearly ninety-six years old, Chantel's sister felt prompted to visit him and ask about his relationship with God. At first, her sister felt the way Chantel felt when her father asked if he could help with the remodel. Her heart said, "No way!" But even as she wrestled with God, her spirit said, "yes." An incredible love washed over her sister, and she drove to visit him.

When she arrived, she didn't waste much time (he was ninety-six, after all). She asked him, point blank, if he had surrendered his life to Jesus. His response shocked her.

"No I haven't," he said, "but I really want to."

So Chantel's sister led their grandfather in the sinner's prayer, and He accepted Jesus as his Savior. A few weeks later, he was baptized. Although he was so frail they had to carry him down into the water, when he rose up from the water he was a brand new man. Now, he's in heaven.

> WHEN WE MAKE THE DECISION TO FORGIVE, AND SURRENDER OUR NEGATIVE FEELINGS TO GOD, HE HEALS OUR HURTS AND GIVES US WHAT WE NEED.

"God is just so good," Chantel told me, when she ended with that part of the story.

The most amazing part of her story, to me, is the way God shaped and shifted her feelings about her grandfather when she surrendered them to Him. She felt anger toward her grandfather, resistance, and even apathy. But when she asked God for what she needed, He gave her love. Perhaps it was this love—totally extravagant, undeserved love—that opened the door to a new eternity.

Surrender Negative Feelings

Just because we have negative feelings toward a person doesn't mean we haven't forgiven them, or that we can't choose to forgive. This used to confuse me. But the more I learn to forgive, and the more women I meet who have offered radical forgiveness, the more I believe it is true. We must choose to forgive *before* the negative feelings go away. It's a decision. When we make the decision to forgive, and surrender our negative feelings to God, He heals our hurts and gives us what we need.

When we relinquish our right to get even, He restores the most broken places. Is there someone you need to forgive? Are you still waiting for it to "feel" right? If forgiveness isn't a feeling, what is it? It is:

- Taking your hurt to God and being honest with Him about how you feel.
- Trusting God to be your defense.
- Praying for the one who hurts you.
- Not returning evil.
- Refusing to get revenge or make the other person pay.
- Not talking to others about it.
- Eventually wanting what is best for the offender.

If you've experienced an offense and you're still hurting, I want to encourage you. God doesn't want you to be harmed in any way. The hurt you experience in response to wrongdoing is a natural response. Don't try to pretend that it doesn't hurt. But let me encourage you not to stay in your place of pain. (Trust me, bitterness is a destructive poison in the heart.) *Choose* to take steps toward forgiveness, and ask God to heal the pain you *feel.*

When you choose to forgive, it says more about *you* than it does about the person you're forgiving. Forgiving says you know you are redeemed, restored, and forgiven. Your feelings will change as you take steps to forgive. Like Chantel, you'll experience a beautiful life.

*   *   *

*"Darkness cannot drive out darkness;
only light can do that. Hate cannot drive
out hate; only love can do that."*

MARTIN LUTHER KING, JR.

CHAPTER TWENTY-ONE

Practical Steps for Forgiveness

"Be completely humble and gentle; be patient,
bearing with one another in love."

EPHESIANS 4:2

W hen I first heard Chantel's story, it made such an impact in my life. I knew forgiveness is possible, and in many ways I knew its power in my life. But seeing it expressed in such an extravagant way was so encouraging. It made me realize forgiveness is not only possible, it's incredibly transformative for everyone involved.

Not only was Chantel's life changed by her choice to forgive, her grandfather's life was changed for eternity, and even *my* life was changed by hearing about it!

In this chapter, I want to share some practical steps to help you navigate your way through forgiveness.

Make a list of people you need to forgive. As you consider the offenses against you, ask God what steps you can take toward forgiveness. Remember, forgiveness is not a feeling. What *actions* do you need to take to forgive?

Pray

The first thing you should do when you need to forgive someone is pray. Notice how Chantel prayed before and during her grandfather's visit. Without God's help, you won't be able to forgive. In prayer, you can take all of your negative feelings (hurt, disappointment, fear) to God. Pray like Chantel did. Ask God to give you exactly what you need. What He gives you might surprise you, but it won't disappoint! Then, after you've prayed for your own heart, don't hesitate to pray in humility for the person who wronged you.

Trust

Trust God to be your advocate. Trust Him to bring justice. Trust Him to care for you in every way. Trust Him to bring redemption to the situation, *beyond* what you could do.

Be Patient

Don't expect results to happen overnight. Galatians 6:9 says, "Let us not become weary in doing good, for at the proper time we will reap a harvest if we do not give up." Not only does forgiveness take time, the healing power of forgiveness takes time. Don't be impatient with yourself if the negative feelings haven't vanished within a few days or weeks. Don't be impatient with the other party if they don't immediately change their mind or their ways.

Just keep trusting, keep obeying, and believe you will "reap a harvest if [you] do not give up."

Make Allowances

People aren't perfect. In fact, most people, most of the time, are doing the best they can. The one who seems like your adversary might not be out to harm you. Remind yourself of this and work to see others as God sees them. This

NOT ONLY DOES FORGIVENESS TAKE TIME, THE HEALING POWER OF FORGIVENESS TAKES TIME.

doesn't mean making allowances for blatant disregard of others; it means making allowances for imperfections. It means we are slow to anger as others are learning and growing.

Give Blessing

The concept of "turning the other cheek" is one of the most challenging of Scripture, yet this is what Jesus did when He sacrificed His life on the cross. He died a death He didn't deserve so we could live a life we didn't earn. What would it look like for us to do the same? I think we could start with blessing those who curse us. Pray good things for your enemy. (If that doesn't take strength of character, I don't know what does.)

Look In a Mirror

We tend to think our response should match the behavior of the one who has offended us (you hit me, I hit you). Or we may even think we should give people what they deserve, but this idea reveals our inadequate understanding of grace. When we act with respect, kindness, and humility, we reveal our character and the work of the Holy Spirit in our lives—not the behavior of the recipient. What do you see when you look at your actions and behavior in a mirror?

> When we forgive, we give God the opportunity to redeem the circumstance.
> #abeautifullife

Root Out Pride

"In your relationships with one another, have the same mindset as Christ Jesus: Who, being in very nature God, did not consider equality with God something to be used to his own advantage; rather, he made himself nothing by taking the very nature of a servant." (Philippians 2:5–7).

Forgiveness is not an option. It's not a feeling. And it isn't easy. But it is a choice, and you can choose it. A choice to step toward forgiveness is a choice to move toward healing, toward heaven, and toward a beautiful life.

•   •   •

"Resentment is like drinking poison and hoping it will kill your enemies."

NELSON MANDELA

Going Deeper
PART SEVEN—FORGIVE AND YOU WILL BE FORGIVEN

DISCUSSION OR JOURNAL QUESTIONS

1. God wants us to forgive. How does a decision not to forgive a person impact our relationship with God? How does it keep us tied to the offense?

2. Forgiveness is not a feeling. How do you surrender those negative feelings to God?

3. There are some very practical steps to take for forgiveness. Read through the steps listed on pages 154–156. Discuss practical ways to take steps in the right direction.

A PERSONAL CHALLENGE

Honestly ask yourself if there is someone you need to forgive. Take a positive step this week toward forgiveness. Consider writing out your thoughts as you process through the journey of forgiveness.

Respect

. . .

In our culture, we're taught to *demand* honor more than we're encouraged to offer it. We're quick to assume people aren't treating us with the respect we "deserve." But how quick are we to think about the respect other people deserve? And how often do we offer respect and honor to those who haven't "earned" it?

Something amazing happens when we choose to honor people, not because of who they are or what they've done, but simply because they're created in the image of God. They become more beautiful. We become more beautiful. God is honored, and His grace is demonstrated in our interactions with others. It isn't easy, but it's truly beautiful.

In the next three chapters, I'll talk a little bit about how to demonstrate respect for others and why it matters so much. I'll share stories of people who have demonstrated great respect to those who didn't earn it. As you read the stories, I think (and pray) you'll see what I see—a life full of respect for others is one worth creating.

CHAPTER TWENTY-TWO

The Way We Respect Others Reveals Our Character

"Show proper respect to everyone."

1 PETER 2:17

A few years ago, I attended a conference with my husband, Mike. The weekend was fun and relaxing, and the speaker had some wonderful things to say. He did a great job delivering his message. By the end of the conference, I felt refreshed and energized. Then, as we were about to check out of the hotel, I saw the conference speaker talking with the concierge.

He asked the concierge a question and, when the young man didn't offer the response he wanted, the speaker raised his voice. I watched from a distance, so I don't know exactly what he said, but I saw the look on his face and watched his body language. I was shocked by what I saw. The confrontation eventually came to an end, and the speaker stomped off, leaving the concierge looking hurt and ashamed.

That image stuck with me for a long time, especially since I had thought so highly of the speaker. Of course, we all have our moments—and I can't judge him based on that one interaction—but I couldn't help thinking how his true character wasn't revealed as he spoke on the platform. It was revealed in how he treated that young man.

> OUR CHARACTER IS TRULY REVEALED IN THE WAY WE RESPECT OTHERS.

We don't often think about respect this way. Many times, we think about respect as something that must be *earned*, something we offer another person when they prove they are worthy. But watching this interaction from a distance, I saw clearly that the speaker's disrespect said more about the *speaker* than it did about the concierge. Even if the concierge made a mistake, he deserved respect—purely on the basis that he is a human being and is loved by God.

This experience was an important reminder for me: *How I treat other people says more about me and my character than it does about the person I'm disrespecting!* If I have a hard time showing respect to those around me, it likely reveals a flaw in *my* character. Not only was this a reminder, it was a wake-up call. It challenged me to examine my actions and ask myself, seriously: "What does my response say about me?"

The next time I was short with my husband, instead of listing a dozen reasons *he* provoked *me*, I considered what my disrespect revealed about my heart. God revealed to me areas where I needed to grow. He uncovered my impatience and my need to have control. Thankfully, He started the process to help me heal and grow in these areas. (Isn't it wonderful that where we are weak, He can make us strong?)

This process is incredibly painful, but incredibly beautiful at the same time. It isn't possible unless we're willing to see the ways our disrespect for others reveals our own character. God meets us in our brokenness, He loves us unconditionally, and He makes us whole again. But none of this can take place until we come before Him in humility and honesty. Our character is truly revealed in the way we respect others.

The Important Role of Humility

If we want an example of someone who gave respect to those who didn't deserve it, we can look at Jesus. Remember when He met Zacchaeus? The book of Luke records the story of a wealthy tax collector (which, in Jesus' day, likely meant he cheated people to make a living). Zacchaeus was desperate to see Jesus, so he rushed to a spot where he knew the teacher would be, and climbed a sycamore tree. The following passage is taken from Luke 19:5–10:

> When Jesus reached the spot, he looked up and said to him, "Zacchaeus, come down immediately. I must stay at your house today." So he came down at once and welcomed him gladly.
>
> All the people saw this and began to mutter, "He has gone to be the guest of a sinner."

But Zacchaeus stood up and said to the Lord, "Look, Lord! Here and now I give half of my possessions to the poor, and if I have cheated anybody out of anything, I will pay back four times the amount."

Jesus said to him, "Today salvation has come to this house, because this man, too, is a son of Abraham. For the Son of Man came to seek and to save the lost."

By all cultural standards, Zacchaeus didn't deserve respect. In spite of that, Jesus wanted to spend time with him and offered him respect. Notice how the people responded. They couldn't believe Jesus would go to the house of a "sinner." They were appalled that Jesus would offer this man undeserved kindness. But Jesus' treatment of Zacchaeus wasn't a reflection of the worthiness of Zacchaeus, it was a reflection of Jesus' character.

Jesus demonstrated this same kind of respect to many others who didn't "deserve" it. He was gracious to the woman caught in adultery, sending her accusers away when they realized they couldn't throw the first stone. He even honored her, drawing the crowd's eyes away from her vulnerable condition by crouching down to the ground to draw something in the sand (John 8:1–11).

He did something similar in His encounter with the woman at the well, who Jesus knew had been married and divorced several times. In her culture, her actions rendered her completely unworthy of respect, but Jesus treated her with dignity and care anyway.

The thief who hung next to Jesus on the cross also received Jesus' respect, although he certainly didn't deserve it. In fact, Jesus gave him the ultimate respect when He said, "Today you will be with me in paradise" (Luke 23:43). Jesus offers that same respect and grace to us. He invites us to accept His free gift of grace and join Him in heaven, not because we are worthy, but because *He* is worthy. His actions say more about Him than they do about us.

> The respect I show reveals my character, not the worthiness of the recipient.
> #abeautifullife

With Jesus as your example, consider your actions toward others as a reflection of your character, rather than the character of those who have harmed you. Are there people you treat with disrespect because you don't believe they deserve better? Consider the people who don't treat you like you "deserve" to be treated. How can you treat them better than they deserve—not as a reflection of their worthiness, but to point to the worthiness of your heavenly Father?

If you find it difficult to show respect to those who don't deserve it, ask God to help you understand why. I've worked with hundreds of women who struggle to respect those who haven't earned it, and the most common reason is old-fashioned pride. (I'm not leaving myself out here—I struggle with pride, too!)

Pride is one of the most difficult sins to recognize in ourselves. What follows is a short list of qualities that reflect humility. Take a look at this list, adapted from Patrick Lencioni's *The Five Dysfunctions of a Team*,[9] and use it as a tool to evaluate yourself. When you're finished, ask yourself: Is pride a problem for me?

Humble people . . .

- Acknowledge their weaknesses.
- Admit their mistakes.
- Are willing to ask for help.
- Accept criticism graciously.
- Give others the benefit of the doubt before arriving at negative conclusions.
- Generously offer feedback and assistance to others.
- Appreciate other's gifts and abilities and tap into them.
- Offer and accept apologies without hesitation.
- Let go of disappointments.
- Cheer others on in their victories.
- Consider how situations make other people feel.

If you struggle with pride, this won't be an easy truth to accept. However, pride is one of the enemy's favorite tactics to keep us from showing respect, which keeps us from a beautiful life. Ask yourself, honestly, if pride is keeping you from treating others with respect. If it is, ask God how you can grow in character and become more humble.

● ● ●

"I speak to everyone in the same way, whether he is the garbage man, or the president of the university."

ALBERT EINSTEIN

CHAPTER TWENTY-THREE

Love God by Being Good to His Children

"The command we have from Christ is blunt:
Loving God includes loving people. You've got to love both."

1 JOHN 4:20, MSG

When I was a young girl, my mom had a friend over to our house for coffee. I greeted her when she arrived, as was the polite thing to do, but then I went about playing with my dolls, more concerned with a childish imagination than with the conversation of adults. I knelt on the kitchen floor, and my mom and her friend sat at the table. They began to talk, and I played quietly.

The two women were only a few minutes into their conversation when my mom's friend stopped mid-sentence.

"Will you get Kerry out of here?" she asked harshly, "I don't want her playing in here while we talk."

I was too young to care about what they were discussing, but I was old enough to know what "get Kerry out of here" and "I don't want her in here" meant. My heart sank. I felt unworthy and disregarded. I'll never forget that feeling; and I never want to make anyone else feel that way.

As I grew older, I realized people wouldn't just treat me differently because of my age. They would also treat me differently if they thought I was somebody important or I had something to offer them. When I began to speak at women's conferences, I was often the "outsider" coming into a close-knit group of women. Since no one recognized my face, at first, I would be for the most part ignored. Then, when someone suddenly realized I was the speaker for the evening, they would lavish me with attention.

Isn't that interesting? Not one thing changed about me from the moment I was ignored to the moment I was treated like a celebrity. Not one thing, except their perception of me.

> WHEN I TREAT PEOPLE AS IF THEY ARE GOD'S CHILDREN, THIS ACTUALLY CHANGES THE WAY I FEEL ABOUT THEM.

But what if we *perceived* every person we met as someone worthy of respect? What if we treated everyone as if they were famous?

When I think of love and respect this way, it changes the way I interact with people. Back in Chapter 6, we discussed the idea of God as a parent. And as a mom, the quickest way to win my heart is to treat my children well. If this is the case, then when we are good to God's children, He is pleased.

When I remember this, I can view every encounter as an opportunity to honor God. When I walk through the check-out line at the grocery store, and learn the name of my clerk—I love Jesus. When I am kind to my husband, despite my bad mood,

I respect Jesus. When a friend comes to my house for coffee, and I make her favorite cake and pull out my nicest mugs, I roll out the red carpet for Jesus.

As if that isn't enough, when I treat people as if they are God's children, this actually changes the way I feel about them. This shouldn't surprise us, considering that our love grows for people when we serve them.

I've heard that we get more of what we celebrate. When we celebrate the image of God in others (even when that image is marred by the residue of sin), we encourage them to become the person He created them to become. It's an amazing, restorative, and beautiful cycle.

How Would You Treat Jesus?

I know this is a challenging idea, but I want to encourage you to think carefully about how you treat people. Consider your family, your spouse, your friends, or complete strangers. How do you treat people who seem to get in your way? Do you treat them with honor and respect? Do you treat them as you would treat Jesus?

My close friend Alex is someone who does this very well, and when I asked her about it, she told me about an incident that impacted her significantly. One day when she was in college, she attended an event with her father. He met a group of friends and stood and talked with them for a few minutes. Wanting to be respectful of their private conversation, she stood behind her father, on the outside of their circle.

When one of the men noticed her standing there, he reached his hand out to introduce himself to her and asked her name. She responded, and he smiled at her and pulled her into the circle.

"Where do you go to school?" He asked, continuing their conversation, with her as part of the group. They talked for just a few minutes, but Alex told me she felt valued and accepted. In a group of men her dad's age, she was the outsider. She was a woman. She was young. Those men didn't *need* to recognize her, and no one would have blamed them if they had continued their conversation without including her. But one man went out of his way to invite her into the group.

When we go out of our way to treat others as we would treat Jesus—when we show them hospitality, when we roll out the red carpet for them, when we treat them even better than they deserve, transformation happens. We become better for it, they become better for it, and—most importantly—Jesus is pleased.

> What if we treated everyone like they were a celebrity?
> #abeautifullife

Treating people differently based on their age, social class, physical appearance, position, or abilities is not the way of Jesus. In fact, I'm certain this grieves Him greatly. Scripture says that "people look at the outward appearance, but the LORD looks at the heart" (1 Samuel 16:7). What would it mean for you to look at the heart of everyone you meet? What if you were to find the image of God in that heart? How would it change the way you treat your daughter, sister, mother, hairstylist, or barista?

God cares about how we treat others—it reveals so much about our hearts and has the ability to impact others in significant ways.

• • •

"People will forget what you say, they'll forget what you do, but they'll never forget how you make them feel."

MAYA ANGELOU

CHAPTER TWENTY-FOUR

The Benefits of a Culture of Honor

"Love one another with brotherly affection.
Outdo one another in showing honor."

ROMANS 12:10, ESV

A few years ago, I met a young woman who had been sexually abused by a family member. The details were heart-wrenching. As a young girl, she was removed from her home and shuffled from one family member to another until she went to college.

Years passed and this young woman became a Christian and got married. She didn't realize how much baggage she was carrying from her past and didn't understand how this would impact her marriage. Before long, she had been unfaithful to her husband on more than one occasion.

After each affair she was remorseful and repentant—and her husband forgave her again and again. When she became pregnant with their first child, she was put on strict bed rest for a portion of her pregnancy, and confined to a hospital room until she delivered the baby.

One day, I went to see her in the hospital and took her a gift. I thought about my own pregnancies, and how rough and dry my feet were, so I thought she would enjoy a pedicure set. I showed up at the hospital, gave her a hug, and handed her a gift. A smile came over her face.

"Oh, thank goodness!" she exclaimed. "My feet are such a mess!"

I was glad she liked it. Then something totally unexpected happened that will stay with me forever. Her father-in-law, who was there with her, said, "Would you like me to put the lotion on your feet? I'd be happy to do that for you."

When I saw how he tenderly treated his daughter-in-law, despite her shortcomings and failures, I realized how powerful it is when we treat people with honor they haven't earned and may not deserve. This man didn't *need* to honor his daughter-in-law in this way—no one expected him to put the lotion on her feet. But he offered anyway, and it was almost like being in the room with Jesus. (I thought of Jesus washing the feet of His betrayer.) That father-in-law showed honor in a visible, tangible way.

When we choose to honor someone—simply because they're made in the image of God—walls fall down, hearts are changed, circumstances are redeemed, people are healed, and God is honored.

> WHAT IF WE ATTACHED HIGH VALUE TO PEOPLE SIMPLY BECAUSE THEY ARE CREATED IN THE IMAGE OF GOD?

What Is Honor and How Does It Work?

Honor is, very simply, attaching high value to a person. Part of the reason this is so counter-intuitive in our culture is that we tend to attach high value to *accomplishments* rather than to people. We attach high honor to status, title, possessions, or position. We honor someone *because* they're successful. We think highly of them because of their status or family background. We might even revere them because they have an interesting job or drive a nice car, rather than honor their personhood.

What if we changed our minds about this? What if we attached high value to people *simply because they are created in the image of God?*

What would happen if the people in your community, workplace, or family stopped trying to outdo one another in accomplishments, and worked instead to outdo one another in showing honor? My guess is the environment would become more positive and productive, the team would grow stronger, and every individual would be given the opportunity to shine. How awesome it would be to change from a culture of competition to a culture of honor!

God wants us to show honor to others. His command to honor our parents has the attached blessing of a long life. Exodus 20:12 says, "Honor your father and your mother, so that you may live long in the land the LORD your God is giving you." Ephesians 6:2–3 reiterates this saying, "'Honor your father and mother'— which is the first commandment with a promise—'so that it may go well with you and that you may enjoy long life on the earth.'"

God is so pleased when we honor one another that He blesses us for it.

What would it take for you to demonstrate honor to others? Are there people on your mind already—your boss, your husband, your children? Perhaps God is reminding you of your parents, or your neighbor, or a distant relative you have not honored. Whoever it is, don't miss this opportunity to change your heart toward that person.

> In every human interaction I have the opportunity either to honor God or to defame Him.
> —Marc Turnage
> #abeautifullife

As you consider how you could show honor to others, don't be surprised if it doesn't come naturally, especially to people who have hurt you deeply. Demonstrating honor to them won't be easy. But let me give you a list of things to help you get started. Here are a few things you can honor about others:

- They were created in the image of God.
- God loves them dearly and sees them as His child.
- They have unique gifts and abilities (you can list specifics).
- They are my _____ (mother, father, sister, aunt, friend, neighbor, etc.).

As you continue on your journey to honor others, keep in mind what you're doing. You're changing the legacy of generations. Based on the truth and reality of Scripture, God will notice your honor and He will bless it. When you demonstrate honor, you help to change hearts, transform circumstances, and heal brokenness. You can change the entire environment of your home, office, or church. You have the power to live a beautiful life—not just for you, but for generations to come.

* * *

"Outdo one another in showing honor."

THE APOSTLE PAUL

Going Deeper
PART EIGHT—RESPECT

DISCUSSION OR JOURNAL QUESTIONS

1. The way we honor and respect others reveals our character. In what ways do our interactions with others reveal what is really in our hearts?

2. Treat everyone as you would treat Jesus. What happens to a child who is treated with honor and respect? Describe how you felt when someone treated you with honor.

3. Consider the benefits of a culture of honor. The English Standard Version translates Romans 12:10 this way: "Love one another with brotherly affection, Outdo one another in showing honor." Wow! Discuss what it would like in your workplace or extended family if everyone tried to outdo one another in showing honor. How does honoring someone reveal the character of Jesus?

A PERSONAL CHALLENGE

Why is pride so difficult to detect in ourselves? Read through the description of humility on page 166 and honestly evaluate where your heart is. Write down areas where you are struggling and take an action step to grow in humility.

PART NINE

Boundaries

• • •

I've intentionally saved this section for the end of the book—
not because what I'm about to discuss is less important than
everything else we've covered, but because it is *so* important.
Love cannot thrive without boundaries. In fact, my guess is that
many of the questions you have after reading the past eight
sections will be answered in the following chapters.

If you've tried to love in the past, and it hasn't felt like a
beautiful experience, I pray you'll linger in this section. I pray
you'll ask God to teach you and show you where your boundaries
might be lacking. If serving doesn't feel joyful to you, if friendships
tend to end in distance and pain, this chapter is for you.

As you read it, I pray you'll uncover deeper, more
satisfying relationships with the people in your life. I pray
you'll be empowered to love extravagantly. May it be a healing
experience—as you walk in this beautiful life.

CHAPTER TWENTY-FIVE

I Am Responsible
for Myself and *to* You

"For we are each responsible for our own conduct."

GALATIANS 6:5, NLT

One time, my husband and I spent a few days in Denver for a conference, and I was totally amazed and overwhelmed by the highway systems. No matter where we drove, there were several lanes of cars on either side of us, speeding past or inching alongside. Knowing how to get from one place to another was difficult; and each time we drove to a new location I felt a bit panicked.

One morning as we drove to the conference, I told my husband how the highway system in Denver felt a little bit like being a pastor's wife.

"What do you mean by that?" he asked.

"Imagine if you were responsible for all the cars on these roads," I began. "What if it was your job to make sure they all had enough gas; clear directions to their destinations; that everyone was getting along; and their cars were in good repair? What if you had to make sure everyone had snacks, each person was comfortable, and no two cars ever got into an accident?"

"There's no way you could do that," Mike said, matter-of-factly.

"Sometimes that's what it feels like to be a pastor's wife. There are just too many people to care for them all. It's too big a job!"

Mike nodded empathetically. "Thankfully, it's not *your job* to take care of them all," he smiled.

In that moment, I realized he was right. Where had the feeling even come from—that I needed to help everyone? The more I thought about it, the more I realized I had taken the message from Galatians 6:2 to heart. We *are* called to "bear one another's burdens." But I had left out verse 5, which declares that "each one should carry their own load."

I don't think I'm alone in my misunderstanding. I think many of us, as women, tend to take care of things that aren't our responsibility—to take on the weight of things that aren't ours to bear.

We're called to bear each other's *burdens,* but not to carry each other's loads. That's an important distinction. A *load* is the weight or responsibility each of us must carry. It includes things like our jobs, our family responsibilities, and our personal commitments. A burden is something different. A burden is something we can't carry by ourselves.[10]

When a husband gets cancer, or a friend loses her job, or a young girl is raped and becomes a single mother—those are burdens people shouldn't have to carry alone. Ultimately, it's God who helps us with our burdens, but He instructs us to help one another carry them.

We aren't called to help everyone. We're called to help those in our community. When Paul urged the Galatians to bear *one another's* burdens, he wasn't asking them to bear all the burdens of the world. That's what Jesus died on the cross for. Paul simply asked them to bear the burdens

> WE'RE CALLED TO BEAR EACH OTHER'S BURDENS, BUT NOT TO CARRY EACH OTHER'S LOADS.

of each other. While you can't make dinner for every person in the world who has had a baby this week, you *can* make dinner for your neighbor.

This distinction was so helpful for me in overcoming the anxieties I felt as a pastor's wife. When we try to bear one another's *loads*, we quickly become weary and discouraged. Not only do we find we don't have the strength to carry the loads of others (the things they're responsible to carry for themselves), we also become frustrated and resentful, as others become demanding and dependent. This is *not* the way of Jesus.

After that discussion on the freeway in Denver, I started to change my mind about what was mine to hold, and what wasn't. God led me to a book called *Boundaries,* by Dr. John Townsend and Dr. Henry Cloud. It taught me how to distinguish between the load that was my responsibility, and the burdens God wanted me to help others bear.

As I began to change my mindset, I found a remarkable shift in perspective. My frustration and anxiety dissipated. My feelings of being overwhelmed nearly disappeared. I actually found I had more love to give than before. Now I was giving it to the right people, in the right way.

Are You Giving Too Much?

It's possible to give too much. I wonder if you might relate with my story. Many women do. Perhaps it's because our hearts are so full of empathy, and we truly want to help those around us who are in need. But when we overstep our boundaries and help too much, we actually don't help at all. Taking someone else's load on yourself—be it your husband, your children, your friend, or your neighbor—isn't loving. It's enabling.

This concept is presented in *Boundaries*. It goes like this: Be responsible *for* yourself and *to* other people. In other words, you are responsible *for* 100 percent of your thoughts, words, actions, and decisions. You are also responsible to show kindness, empathy, love, and compassion to those around you. You are *not* responsible for *their* thoughts, actions, decisions, or feelings.[11]

This sounds nice when it's written in a book, but in real life situations, it can get messy, so I want to give you a few examples.

Let's say your friend has a car accident. She only has liability insurance, and doesn't have much money. The car is totaled, and she no longer has transportation.

In this circumstance, you are responsible *to* your friend. You are responsible to be kind to her, to be understanding, to have compassion. You can empathize with her circumstance. But you are not responsible *for* her mistake. You're not responsible to buy her a new car, to pick her up for work every morning, or to pay for her bus ticket. You might choose to do any one of those things for a period of time out of your concern for her, but ultimately, only she can take responsibility for her mistake.

This message is congruent with Scripture, which expects each person to bear his or her own load. Proverbs 13:4 speaks strongly against the sluggard and 1 Thessalonians 2:10 clearly states that those who don't work, won't eat. Sadly, many times this message gets lost or distorted. There's a widespread misunderstanding about the importance of boundaries within the Christian community.

One of the reasons boundaries are so important to God is that, when we make others dependent on us, we steal the joy they can find when they depend on the Holy Spirit. Think about this the next time you feel guilty for saying no to someone who asks for your help. Ask yourself if by helping that person, you might be stepping in where *God* wants to help them.

> We become weary and discouraged when we take on things we are not meant to carry.
> #abeautifullife

Are boundaries something you struggle with? If you aren't sure, I can give you a quick test. The symptoms of violated boundaries are things like anxiety, anger, and constant feelings of stress or frustration. If your temper is short, or you frequently feel burdened or resentful, you might need to work on setting better boundaries in your life.

If you tend to accept responsibilities that aren't yours, I encourage you to make a list of things you are responsible for. Include some of the major roles in your life, and even a few descriptive words about what it means to fulfill those roles:

What am I responsible for?

- My thoughts
- My attitudes
- My behaviors
- My actions
- My words
- My responses

I am a wife . . .

I am the overseer of my home . . .

I am a mother . . .

I am a daughter . . .

I am an employee . . .

I am a supervisor . . .

With this list of responsibilities in hand, you won't have to feel guilty for saying no to unrealistic expectations. Boundaries make God happy. Boundaries usher in a beautiful life.

•   •   •

*"I used to want to fix people, but now
I just want to be with them."*

BOB GOFF

CHAPTER TWENTY-SIX

Be Careful Where You Entrust Yourself

"Discretion will protect you, and understanding will guard you."

PROVERBS 2:11

O ur culture places a lot of emphasis on authenticity and, in one sense, that's a good thing. When we're truthful with ourselves and others, God is pleased and our lives become more beautiful. But I fear for the hundreds of women I've met who misunderstand what it means to be authentic. Authenticity does not mean you must share all things with all people.

In the last chapter we discussed the importance of boundaries, and I mentioned that boundaries make God happy because they teach others to rely on the Holy Spirit. There's another reason good boundaries make God happy: They protect us from unnecessary harm.

When Mike and I were first engaged, he worked at a bank where he was the only male employee. Day after day, while he worked with the women at the bank, he heard them speak negative and inappropriate words about their husbands and their marriages. Often, he thought to himself, *Why are they sharing this information with me?*

One day, after a particularly negative conversation, he asked if we could make an important promise to each other.

"Can we decide we will never talk negatively about each other to other people like that?" I agreed, and we've kept that promise to each other ever since.

I still shake my head every time I think of those women. They were crossing a line and damaging their relationships to each other, to their husbands, and to Mike. It was truly the opposite of beautiful.

Not only did those women embarrass themselves by sharing information that was inappropriate for a professional setting, they shared information with people who were not safe keepers of secrets. Consider the irony of this. Each woman was airing her husband's dirty laundry to a group of women who were gossiping and slandering. What do you suppose would happen when a woman in the group demonstrated a less-than-attractive quality about herself? She would become the victim of gossip herself!

Mike never felt safe to share any personal information with these women—and rightfully so. He was authentic with them, but rarely shared any information that wasn't necessary for their working relationship. This is what it looks like to have good boundaries.

Unfortunately, good boundaries don't come easy. In fact, setting emotional boundaries seems to be particularly difficult for women. I've been in Bible studies where a woman comes in and shares the deepest secrets of her marriage during her first visit. It feels cathartic for her, but for everyone else, it's uncomfortable. Rather than receive the affirmation she longs for, the other women in the group withdraw in embarrassment.

It's so important to consider carefully where we entrust ourselves.

I commonly meet women who open up to people they aren't sure are trustworthy. I can't tell you how often I meet women who tell me their entire life stories within the first five minutes of knowing me. I enjoy meeting women and hearing about their struggles, and I consider myself a trustworthy person. But my heart worries for these women. They aren't using discretion about where and how to share their deepest secrets.

> IT'S SO IMPORTANT TO CONSIDER CAREFULLY WHERE WE ENTRUST OURSELVES.

Author Jodi Detrick says it's possible to be authentic with everyone, while being transparent with a few.[12] This is a small distinction, but an important one. By authenticity, I mean being the same kind of person, no matter the setting. Whether she's at work, at school, with family or friends, a woman who reflects consistent character qualities—the same fruit of the Spirit—is an authentic woman.

When this woman is at church, she is gracious and kind. When she's at the office, she's gracious and kind. When she speaks with her children, she's gracious and kind. What this doesn't mean is that she shares the same information or intimacy with her coworkers, her children, her husband, and her pastor. Authenticity and transparency are two different things.

Transparency, unlike authenticity, isn't simply about reflecting the same character traits in every setting. It's about allowing someone to see into the private places of your heart and mind. Transparency isn't a bad thing. It's just safest and most satisfying when it's reserved for a few trustworthy people.

I meet women all the time who are confused about this, and their confusion is causing them tremendous pain. In one sense they feel forced to be vulnerable with everyone. In another sense, they don't feel safe to be vulnerable with anyone. They don't evaluate what information to share and what to keep private. They end up hurt, betrayed, taken advantage of, and sucked into the trap of gossip.

To me, that's not a beautiful life. But another way is possible.

Who Is Trustworthy?

One of the most difficult parts about this conversation, for me, is that many women aren't sure how to entrust themselves in relationships. They don't know who is safe or trustworthy. Teaching people how to discern when someone is safe can be a bit tricky because each circumstance and situation is different.

One rule of thumb to determine if someone is trustworthy is this: past behavior is indicative of future behavior. In other words, if someone gossips to you about another friend, chances are that person will eventually go to someone else and gossip about you. If you share a secret with a friend, and she doesn't keep that secret, I would advise not sharing secrets with her. This principle can help you make wise decisions about what safe relationships should look like.

This leads me to my second rule of thumb, which is simply that relationships should have different levels of transparency and intimacy. My relationship with my husband, for example, is extremely close. We share everything with one another. We are completely transparent. My relationships with my coworkers, on the other hand, are different. I have a tightknit group of coworkers I share life with, but not at the same level of transparency I share with Mike.

Consider flipping back to Chapter 7 for a minute, and thinking about the variety of relationships in your life. Who are the people you're closest to? Is it your husband? A friend? A sister? If you're withholding pieces of yourself from those people, my guess is, you feel very lonely. God wants us to have trustworthy people in our lives with whom we can be honest.

> It is possible and important to be yourself with everyone, while sharing your secrets with a few. #abeautifullife

Now, if you told me your closest relationship was with your teenage daughter, and you were completely transparent with her, I would be concerned. Is your daughter able to process the information you're giving her? Has she been given the grace to hold your burden? Should that be her role? I would argue no. Transparent relationships are good, but we need to be wise about who shares those relationships with us.

My final rule of thumb for those who struggle to set positive boundaries is this: When you try to set boundaries in your life, the enemy will tempt you to stop. He'll whisper things to you like, "You don't deserve what you're asking for" or "You're being rude if you don't answer." Ignore those lies. You never need to feel guilty for dealing cautiously with your heart. Ask the Holy Spirit to guide you in making these decisions and to teach you how to be cautious.

Good boundaries don't just make God happy, they make us happy and healthy, too. They help us go about our beautiful lives.

•   •   •

"Boundaries help us keep the good in, and the bad out."

DR. HENRY CLOUD

CHAPTER TWENTY-SEVEN

Don't Wear Out
Your Welcome

"Seldom set your foot in your neighbor's house—
too much of you, and they will hate you."

PROVERBS 25:17

S everal years ago, I had an experience that taught me why it's important to learn good boundaries, not just with ourselves but with each other. I was leading a Bible study and one of the women in the group—Melinda—asked if we could meet for coffee. We did, and at coffee she told me a heart-wrenching story about her childhood. Pretty much everything unimaginable that could have happened to her, did.

My heart broke as she told me the details, and I wanted to do anything I could to help her. So I offered her my cell phone number, as well as my email, and I told her to call anytime she needed. The problem is, when I said that, I didn't realize what I was offering. By the end of the day, I had dozens of missed calls and voicemails from her, and by the end of the week I had nearly a hundred emails.

As much as I wanted to help my new friend, there was no way I could keep up with that kind of communication. On top of that, I feared the help I could give her wouldn't be the kind she truly needed.

Later that week, I called Melinda and asked if she could meet me for coffee again. She agreed. I told her, cautiously but directly, "Melinda, I can't talk on the phone with you several times in a day. What I *can* do is talk with you once each week for thirty minutes. How does that sound?"

Melinda thought about it for a minute, and I waited patiently for her response. After looking at the floor for a few seconds, she looked back at me.

"How about forty-five minutes?" she asked.

Personal Boundaries

That interaction with Melinda makes me laugh a little, even now as I write about it. I grew to love Melinda and she grew to love me, but the only way our relationship was possible was with strong personal boundaries.

We all have people in our lives like Melinda. They can be a huge drain on our time and energy if we let them. The truth is that women *everywhere* struggle with personal boundaries. Chances are good you'll meet people who overstay their welcome in your home or in your life. (You might even be one of those people!) But rather than complain about them or gossip about them, let's learn a few strategies to help us maintain strong boundaries in spite of their unhealthy habits. Here are some steps you can take to create strong personal boundaries. They are adapted from the book I mentioned earlier, *Boundaries.*

IDENTIFY THE SYMPTOM. In my case with Melinda, the symptom was dozens of missed phone calls and emails. When I suggested that she "call me anytime," I never considered she would take it to the extreme. So when the symptom appeared, I was certain I had a problem. Look around your own life and identify "symptoms" of bad boundaries. These symptoms are probably areas where you feel frustrated or feel you have lost control of what Dr. Cloud calls "personal property."[13]

> BOUNDARIES TAKE PRACTICE, AND THE MORE I PRACTICE, THE BETTER MY BOUNDARIES GET.

IDENTIFY THE CONFLICT. The conflict with Melinda wasn't that she called so often. It was that I couldn't talk to her that often. What she wanted and what I was able to offer were not the same. So something had to change. When people make unrealistic demands on you, consider carefully and objectively what you're willing to offer. Then identify the conflict between what you can offer and what that person hopes to receive.

IDENTIFY THE NEED THAT CAUSES THE CONFLICT. Needs on both sides of the relationship contribute to the conflict. In my case, Melinda needed to talk to someone about some serious emotional issues she was dealing with. That was a real need, and one she shouldn't be ashamed of. At the same time, I needed to do my job (which wasn't a therapist) and I had to be honest about the fact that I couldn't help her in the way she needed. If you catch yourself thinking that others aren't living up to your expectations, identify the need you have that is pushing you to that place. Do you need community? Love? Attention? Affection? Do you know that God can meet those needs for you?

TAKE IN AND RECEIVE THE GOOD. This is an important step because some women might have identified the symptom or the conflict with Melinda and then rejected her completely. In fact, I know many other women who did this (and trust me, I almost did the same myself). Their rejection didn't help her. In fact, it only made the problem worse. No matter how confusing or dire your circumstances seem, find the good and hold onto it—the way I held onto the good with Melinda.

> If people can't set the right boundaries in their relationships with you, you must set the limits for them.
> #abeautifullife

PRACTICE BOUNDARY SKILLS. This story makes me look like I have perfect boundaries, but I promise you, I don't. Boundaries take practice, and the more I practice, the better my boundaries get. This conversation with Melinda wasn't my first one like it. If you struggle with boundaries in your life, don't beat yourself up over it. Just consider it something God wants to teach you. Start implementing your boundary skills (like those listed here). Practice makes perfect.

SAY NO TO THE BAD. As I advised in the last chapter, avoid harmful situations. This is why I met Melinda at a coffee shop, rather than at my office or home. I wanted to meet her in a public place so she would be less likely to act inappropriately.

RESPOND, DON'T REACT. The reason I didn't call Melinda back after her tenth phone call and give her a piece of my mind was that I was taking time to *respond* appropriately to her. With a little bit of time and distance, I was able to think objectively about what I wanted to say to her and what I could realistically offer. When you find yourself reacting to circumstances—intentionally walk yourself through the tips on this list and practice those boundary skills.

LEARN TO LOVE IN FREEDOM AND RESPONSIBILITY, NOT GUILT. Love that is free of guilt is the purest kind of love. Love that says to Melinda, "I'm offering to meet with you for thirty minutes a week, no strings attached" is even more valuable than the love that says, "Okay, fine, we can talk every day, but you better be grateful!" Learn to love freely. Be responsible *to* others without being responsible *for* them. And enjoy the beauty of guilt-free, overflowing, joyful love in your life.

*   *   *

"When you are dealing with someone who is hurting, remember your boundaries are both necessary for you and helpful for them."

DR. HENRY CLOUD

Going Deeper
PART NINE—BOUNDARIES

DISCUSSION OR JOURNAL QUESTIONS

1. I am responsible *for* myself and *to* you. What happens when we begin to think that we're responsible for each other? Read the list of things we're each responsible for on page 186, How can we stayed focused on those things and not accept responsibilities we were never meant to carry?

2. Be careful where you entrust yourself. What are the differences between transparency and authenticity? (This is found on pages 189–190.) Why is it important to be authentic with everyone and transparent with only a few?

3. Don't wear out your welcome. Discuss practical ways to establish personal boundaries with people who have trouble understanding they need them? (This is found on pages 195–197.)

A PERSONAL CHALLENGE

Take time to evaluate your personal boundaries. Consider writing out your responses to the following questions and make some personal goals for areas where you need improvement. Are you responsible for yourself and to others? Or are you trying to change others while neglecting to take control of your own responsibilities? Are you the same in every circumstance? Do you know the appropriate levels of transparency with the different individuals in your life? Do you have healthy boundaries with others to respect personal time and space?

The Power of Presence

• • •

It feels right to end this book talking about the power of presence. Loving others can be complicated. It can be difficult. It can be confusing. But it can also be really simple. Sometimes, all we need to do to love someone is to be there. Whether someone is grieving, rejoicing, or simply needing a friend—one of the most powerful things we can do is be with them.

Not only is presence impactful, it is a reflection of how God reveals His love for us. He promises never to leave us. And when we were "yet sinners," Romans 5:8 tells us, God sent His only Son to earth to *be with* us. He didn't try to love us from afar. He came close.

Do you know we can do this too? Do you realize that when we come close to someone who is hurting or rejoicing, when we are just *with* them, we bring God with us. This is why it says in Matthew 18:20, "Where two or three gather in my name, there am I with them." God is omnipresent (meaning He is always present), but in many ways, God's loving presence follows our presence.

As you read this final section, consider how your simple presence in someone's life could make their life more beautiful. Consider how it could make yours more beautiful. Ask God where He is urging you to be present.

CHAPTER TWENTY-EIGHT

A Time to Cry

"Mourn with those who mourn."

ROMANS 12:15

C an you think of a time when you were so upset—so deep in grief—that you didn't know which way was up? A time when you felt as if an ocean wave had tumbled over you and was pulling you out to sea? I can remember only a few times when I felt that way, and this was one of them.

My father is a musician, and he traveled often to play for different churches. One particular weekend, he was playing at a church in Missouri when the unthinkable happened. He was in the middle of setting up his equipment when he collapsed into his guitar case. The pastor of the church leapt into action.

"Does anyone know CPR?" he yelled, and someone from the audience raised his hand. This man was a first-time visitor to the church, but he was a trained CPR instructor. He raced to the front of the room where my dad was lying.

For twenty minutes this man gave my dad CPR. There was no heartbeat, but while the paramedics were on their way, this complete stranger worked hard to keep my dad alive. Still, by the time my mother called and told us the news, she was certain Dad was gone.

"There's no heartbeat," was all she could say.

We raced to the hospital, where the physicians put Dad on ice to lower his body temperature and preserve his organs since his heart had been stopped for so long. They got his heart beating again, but he was in intensive care. Nine long days passed with little change. As far as I was concerned, we were on a death watch.

There's nothing more painful than believing something awful is going to happen, and just waiting for it to take place. I don't know if you've ever had this experience—expecting the death of a family member, or a divorce, or the slow loss of a friend to cancer. Yet, in spite of the great pain I felt during the nine days Dad was in intensive care, the power of presence was completely amazing.

WE NEED TO GET GOOD AT HELPING PEOPLE FIND THEIR WAY THROUGH GRIEF!

People came. From all over the place, from every part of our life, they came. They brought blankets, food, and things we didn't ask for but desperately needed. It was such a powerful time. Although we should have felt stressed, we really didn't. We were so well cared for. The power of presence carried us through our trauma.

The experience of almost losing my dad taught me that I don't have to fear death. Ultimately, I don't have to fear death because of the power of the presence of God. But it also taught me how powerful it can be to have people with you while you are grieving, afraid, or confused. That is a gift I don't want to keep to myself. That is a gift I want to give generously to others.

Helping a Friend Through Grief

Have you ever had a friend in a difficult situation and you didn't know what to do? Grief doesn't come only with death; it can come with the loss of a job, the loss of a dream, or the loss of financial stability. Major life changes often bring grief. We need to get good at helping people find their way through grief!

Being *with* those who are grieving can be difficult and uncomfortable, since we don't know exactly what to say, but chances are you don't need to say anything. God has loved me, in my darkest hours, through the presence of friends and family. They didn't say anything profound or do anything amazing. They were just there—like God would be—loving me unconditionally.

When people lose someone they love, they first need to turn to friends and family members for support. At one time or another each one of us will need to help a friend who has lost a loved one. Here are some things you can do, and some things you should not do, to help your friend recover and heal.

DO THESE THINGS:

1. Initially, your friend needs tangible expressions of your support. Give her a hug and be present as she first copes with her loss.

2. Next, she and her family members will need physical care. Coordinate volunteers to bring food to provide variety and quantity. Consider bringing disposable items as well, such as paper plates, napkins, cups, and disposable containers of food so the grieving family doesn't have to worry about returning empty dishes to owners.

3. Help keep a list of incoming food, plants, and other items, so the family can send thank-you notes later.

4. Offer to answer the phone, take messages, or even make phone calls to announce the difficult news so the family is relieved of that responsibility.

5. Oversee household responsibilities as needed. Laundry, cleaning, picking up incoming guests at the airport or bus station, caring for pets, paying bills, or offering child care are all tangible ways to help the grieving family.

6. Offer to help with the funeral arrangements as needed. A friend can help organize photos, gather music, write the obituary, or run necessary errands to help relieve the stress on the family.

7. Experts say that those dealing with emotional pain need to hear something emotionally satisfying and something intellectually satisfying to help them cope. Don't force your friend to talk about her loss if she's not ready, but invite her to express her feelings by asking, "Do you feel like talking?" Accept and acknowledge her feelings; be willing to sit in silence with her, or let her talk about her loved one who died. You can offer comfort without minimizing her loss.

8. Do say these things:

   a. I'm sorry for your great loss.

b. I'm praying for you, and I care that you hurt.

c. I can't imagine the pain you feel.

d. I am here for you. Whatever I can do to ease your pain, please let me know.

> We weren't created to mourn alone— mourning should be done in community. #abeautifullife

9. Continue to help your friend and her family for six months to one year after the loss of their loved one. Call to remind her you are praying for her, take her on an outing, acknowledge her special days (the birthday of the deceased, an anniversary, and first holidays without the loved one), accompany her to the gravesite, or listen as she cries.

10. In the coming days and weeks, watch for signs that your friend may have moved into clinical depression, such as confusion, disconnection from others, or symptoms of grief that become worse. Encourage your friend to seek professional help if you see: difficulty functioning in daily life, inability to enjoy life, extreme focus on death, withdrawal, hallucinations, neglecting personal hygiene, hopelessness, or talk of suicide. In extreme cases, you can call a suicide hotline or 9-1-1.

AVOID DOING THESE THINGS:

1. Avoid minimizing the loss. Let the grieving person work through her emotions by talking it through with you, without you minimizing the loss, or brushing it away. Avoid

saying something like, "You know, we all lose someone." Or, "You're going to have to get over this."

2. Don't make the grieving person validate her grief. Again, let the griever talk through her grief. She shouldn't feel the need to say something like: "I know I should be past this grief by now." Accept her where she is in her journey, and let her grieve at her own pace. Each situation is different, so there is no timetable for recovery.

3. Don't use the following clichés when speaking to a bereaved person:

   a. This is all part of God's plan.

   b. You need to be strong. Others are counting on you.

   c. I know how you feel.

   d. Your loved one is in a better place now.

   e. This is behind you. It's time to get on with your life.

   f. Avoid statements that begin with "You should . . ." or "You will . . ."; try rephrasing your comments to, "Have you thought about . . ." or "You might try . . ."[14]

None of us can take the pain or loss from someone else, but we can help our grieving friend know that we care.

●   ●   ●

"Tell me how much you know of the sufferings of your fellow man; and I will tell you how much you have loved them."

HELMUT THIELICKE

CHAPTER TWENTY-NINE

Celebrate Good Times (Come on!)

"Rejoice with those who rejoice."

ROMANS 12:15A

O ne Sunday, after church, I went to use the restroom. Of course, the church bathroom was packed with women, the way it tends to be right after Sunday service. Nikki, a young girl about nine-years-old at the time, was in the bathroom that morning.

When I walked into the bathroom, I noticed that the door was sticking. "Oh, wow, this door is really sticking!" I said out loud.

"You should tell Pastor Mike about that," Nikki said, referring to my husband.

"Why should I tell him, Nikki?" I asked, smiling.

"Because he owns the church!" She exclaimed.

"Oh honey, *Jesus* owns the church," I laughed, not wanting her to think my husband owned the church.

"Well," she continued, "I still think you should tell Pastor Mike, because Jesus ain't gonna fix that door!"

The entire restroom of women burst into laughter; it was such a sweet moment. But I think Nikki was actually onto something profound. Although Jesus is the "owner" of the church, so to speak, there are still some things *we* must do.

To me, this comment beautifully expresses how we are called to be the hands and feet of Jesus. When it comes to "fixing a door" (bringing a meal to a friend, throwing a party, giving the gift of encouragement, creating opportunities for fun and laughter) how many of us are waiting for Jesus to take care of it, when it's *our* responsibility?

> When we take every opportunity to celebrate goodness, we are building a beautiful life. #abeautifullife.

What Are Some Simple Ways to Celebrate with People?

I don't know about you, but celebrations sometimes feel like they make my life more complicated, rather than more fun. But I don't believe this was God's intention. The festivals prescribed in the Old Testament were a time to remember God's goodness and to rejoice. Sabbath was a gift from God, a time to rest in His provision and celebrate the work He had equipped us to do. Part of the reason I think celebration can feel difficult is because we make it more complicated than it needs to be.

I'm reminded of what I shared in Chapter 13: "Biblical Hospitality Has Nothing to Do with Martha Stewart." Sometimes I think we get caught up in the outward appearance of celebration rather than the true meaning of rejoicing with others. The purpose of celebration is not to have the fanciest food, or the most beautiful decorations. The purpose is to rejoice in God's goodness and make an individual feel celebrated. This is so much easier than we realize.

Here are some easy ways to celebrate those in your life.

- **Give a compliment.** This is really simple, but celebration can be as easy as telling someone what a great job they did planning the winter carnival, or how good they look in that sweater. Give a compliment today and watch how someone's face changes right in front of you.
- **Give a simple gift.** Oftentimes we focus on giving extravagant gifts, and it can become overwhelming to find something that will impress. What if we simply stopped by a friend's house and brought her a vase of flowers? The simplest gifts can be the most thoughtful and heartfelt.
- **Notice and validate strengths.** Sometimes simply noticing where someone is gifted can make them feel acknowledged and celebrated. It can be something as simple as, "Wow, you're really gifted with children! You handled that situation so well."

- **Know their favorites.** What would happen
  if you brought a friend their favorite drink,
  candy bar, snack, or color of nail polish? There's
  something powerful about knowing a person's
  favorite things and treating them to something
  they love.
- **Plan an outing.** When your friend gets a new job,
  announces a move, or discovers she's going to have
  a baby, take her to dinner, to get a pedicure, or just
  to get a cup of coffee. Planning a specific outing
  commemorates the moment and lets her know you
  care about the event as much as she does.
- **Look for opportunities.** Don't wait for
  birthdays or anniversaries to celebrate. Look for
  opportunities to celebrate. I have a friend who
  celebrates her children's half-birthdays by baking
  half a cake. Celebrate things like your husband's
  successful business meeting, your child's report
  card, or the longest day of the year.
- **Plan rest.** Taking time to rest can be a
  celebration. After a busy season, or in the middle
  of a busy season, plan time to slow down and help
  others slow down, too.
- **Keep notes in your smartphone.** Pay attention
  to the kind of coffee your friend orders or to a
  book she says she would love to read. Keep the
  notes in your smartphone. Next time you swing
  by a coffee shop or a bookstore, you'll know
  exactly what will make her day!

- **Express gratitude.** Life moves so fast we
  sometimes forget to tell people how thankful we
  are for the gifts they bring into our lives. It can be
  as simple as their smile, their laughter, or more
  overt—like the time they picked you up when
  your car broke down. Express gratitude often.

It's amazing how simple and inexpensive genuine celebration can be! It's all about paying attention to the details and hearing what's going on in the lives of those around you.

Celebrating with others can be as powerful as mourning with them. I believe this is why Paul commands us to do it. When we celebrate the good things in our lives and the beauty of other people, God smiles.

Celebration changes people. Watch how a woman's defenses melt, how she becomes more vulnerable and easier to be around, how her countenance changes when she feels

> WHEN WE CELEBRATE THE GOOD THINGS IN OUR LIVES AND THE BEAUTY OF OTHER PEOPLE, GOD SMILES.

celebrated. And when you celebrate *with* others *you* change, too. You become more beautiful, the people around you become more beautiful, and the life you're living becomes a beautiful life.

Celebration also changes environments. Think about the last time you were in a group of people who were comparing, judging, and gossiping. What was that environment like? My guess is it was full of jealousy and fear, and no one enjoyed being there. Work environments can be like this, home environments

can be like this, school or church environments can be like this—
and they're toxic.

On the other hand, think of a time when those around you
recognized God's goodness and you felt celebrated for what you
brought to the table. Maybe it was a friend who took you out to
celebrate your birthday. Perhaps it was a boss who went out of
his way to thank you for your hard work. Or, maybe it was your
husband stopping to say, "You're so good at what you do. Thank
you for making dinner." The beneficial environment created by
celebration is the opposite of toxic.

We were made to celebrate. Think about Christmas with
the wonder and awe you felt as a little girl, watching the lights
glisten on the Christmas tree. It is the season of Advent, waiting
to celebrate Christ's birth. What if we thought of all celebration
as worship—recognizing and rejoicing in God's goodness? That
would truly be a beautiful life!

Are You Good at Celebrating?

If you want to know how good you are at celebrating with others,
spend some time scrolling through Facebook. That sounds like a
joke, but I'm serious. My friend Justin says that our tendency
to scroll through Facebook and compare ourselves to others,
tearing them down in our hearts, doesn't reflect a problem with
Facebook. It reflects a problem with us. I agree with him.

Jealousy and comparison are some of the most toxic
attitudes we can adopt and yet, tragically, they are some of the
most common. If you find yourself scrolling through Facebook,
comparing yourself to others—what they have, what they wear,

where they've been, what they've been doing—don't simply quit Facebook. That doesn't solve the problem. Ask God to help you understand why you have a hard time celebrating with others.

If you struggle with jealousy and comparison, you're not alone. Seek to find the root of the problem so you can stop suffering the consequences. God wants something so much better for you! Jealousy and comparison are damaging to our souls. They prevent us from celebrating our own strengths, and from celebrating the strengths of others.

Celebrating with others is good for us! Recently I read Andy Stanley's book, *Enemies of the Heart.* He says that celebrating with others is a way to guard our hearts against jealousy.[15] As we rejoice with others about the good things God is doing in their lives, we prevent envy from taking a destructive hold in our thoughts. So do something good for others and yourself—throw a party, give a compliment, or validate someone's talents!

*   *   *

"People are drawn to where they are celebrated."

UNKNOWN

CHAPTER THIRTY

The Gift of Presence

"God of all healing and counsel! He comes alongside us
when we go through hard times, and before you know it, he
brings us alongside someone else who is going through
hard times so that we can be there for that
person, just as God was there for us."

2 CORINTHIANS 1:4, MSG

I like to be busy. I function best when my schedule is full and
I'm accomplishing a lot. But every once in awhile, I overdo
it, and I find myself overwhelmed and unhappy. Whenever this
happens, I have a few friends who are healing to be around.

Usually, if I'm overwhelmed, it's because work has
been busy. Maybe I've worked long hours, experienced tight
deadlines, or had many situations to fill my time. Like you, I can
feel exhausted. On those days, I don't expect anyone to fix the
situation. But there's something healing about a long lunch and
meaningful conversation with a close friend.

At first glance, it would seem like the last thing I need when I have too much to do is to take an hour out of my day to go to lunch. But every single time this happens I'm shocked by how much it changes my attitude. Usually it starts with the question, "How are you today, Kerry?" And although I try to downplay how overwhelmed I really am, those closest to me can see right through it.

One simple hour in the presence of a good friend—being listened to, acknowledged, valued and heard—and I leave the restaurant a new woman. I'm happier, more focused, less overwhelmed. Encouraged! *That's the power of presence.*

Have you ever experienced what I'm talking about—the simple act of being *with* a friend actually helps you to feel better? The gift of presence is no small gift. It can change someone's life.

A Beautiful Life

I can't think of any subject I'd rather use to close a book about love, a book about a beautiful life, than the power of presence. To me, this sums up the entire book in just a few words. We were created to be in relationship—relationship with God and relationship with each other—and relationship doesn't need to be as complicated as we sometimes make it. Sometimes, it can just be about *being there.*

This is how God demonstrated His love for us. He was present, even while we were still sinners, even when we didn't deserve it, even when we weren't fun to be around. This is how good parents love their children, by being consistent with them, continuing to show up over and over, no matter what their child's response. This is how good friends treat us. They are just with us. They don't try to fix us. They just show up. They sit with us. They listen.

There is something so healing about being with someone.

Remember my friend Carol, from Chapter 1? This is what her young son wanted in the last days of his life—to be surrounded by those that he loved. This is what changed Becky's life, my friend from Chapter 3. It wasn't preaching or counseling that changed her. It was berry-picking with a friend. That's the power of presence.

The power of presence was what I needed when I found out my son had Congenital Hip Dysplasia (Chapter 4). It's also what I offered the difficult young woman from my Bible study in Chapter 8, and she felt loved.

Love is demonstrated and received in the power of presence, the way my friend Ally traveled to be *with* the people of Guatemala, and her experience didn't just bless the villagers, it changed her perspective forever (Chapter 13); or my friend Ariel who decided to be *with* her friend, the former worship leader, and found her friendship didn't just soften her heart and release her from her own bitterness, but also deeply blessed her.

> THERE IS SOMETHING SO HEALING ABOUT BEING WITH SOMEONE.

How about Chapter 21, when Chantel's willingness to invite her grandfather back into her home—her simple agreement to be *with* him—changed the entire dynamic of the family and ended with her grandfather in heaven? If that isn't a powerful example of presence, I don't know what is.

I could go on and on, but I think you get the picture. When we are simply *with* people, we can love them. When we love others, Jesus is happy, and so are we.

At this point in the book, I would be doing a disservice if I didn't urge you to take an honest look at your life. Is it a beautiful one, or do you still have work to do? I, for one, still have work to do. And I'm not about to give up on building it.

> When I live a beautiful life, it leaves a beautiful fragrance behind. It makes the lives of others more beautiful, too.
> #abeautifullife

I want to be remembered for my love. I want to bring God's love to earth. And the only way to do that is to invest in people, to be with them, to give them my time and energy, and to love them well.

This makes God happy. But even more than that, it makes us happy too. I think sometimes we think those two things are separate—that to make God happy we have to be unhappy—but I would argue, more often than not, our happiness and God's happiness are found in the same place.

With every thought of you I have prayed that as you learn to apply these truths, you will experience *a beautiful life!*

• • •

"When we love each other, God smiles and our hearts rejoice. We really are living a beautiful life."

KERRY CLARENSAU

Going Deeper
PART TEN—THE POWER OF PRESENCE

DISCUSSION OR JOURNAL QUESTIONS

1. There is a time to cry. Read through the Do's and Don'ts of Grief found on pages 205–208. Discuss the benefits of mourning in a community of friends and family.

2. We should celebrate together! Someone once said that people are drawn to where they are celebrated. Share a time when a celebration had a significant impact on your life. Share simple ideas for celebrating with those you love.

3. You can offer the gift of presence. Consider the ways you've been encouraged when someone spent time with you. How can you give the gift of your presence to someone else?

A PERSONAL CHALLENGE

Read through the easy ways to celebrate those in your life and decide one way to "celebrate" someone in your life this week. If someone you know is grieving, take time to grieve with that person.

How to Use *A Beautiful Life* with Small Groups

. . .

T his book can be used in a ten-week small group study. Each of the ten parts of this book contains three short chapters. Consider reading one part for each weekly session. Use the questions on the Going Deeper pages at the end of each part, or your own questions, to guide the discussion. Encourage each participant to purchase a journal and accept the weekly personal challenges. You may want to start your time together each week by allowing the participants to share their stories of engaging in the personal challenges.

Notes

* * *

1. Caroline Leaf, PhD, *Who Switched Off My Brain?: Controlling Toxic Thoughts and Emotions* (Nashville: Thomas Nelson, Inc.), 120.

2. Allan N. Schore, *Affect Regulation and the Repair of the Self* (New York: W. W. Norton and Company, 2003).

3. Leaf, *Who Switched Off My Brain?*, 87.

4. Tom Holladay, *The Relationship Principles of Jesus* (Grand Rapids, MI: Zondervan, 2008), 90, 292.

5. L. M. Montgomery, *Anne of Green Gables* (New York: Bantam Books, 1982), 217.

6. Ken Sande, *The Peacemaker: A Biblical Guide to Resolving Personal Conflict* (Grand Rapids, MI: Baker books, 2004), 83.

7. Norman Shawchuck, *How to Manage Conflict in the Church, Understanding and Managing Conflict* (Fargo, ND: Spiritual Growth Resources, 1983).

8. Jim Van Yperen, *Making Peace: A Guide to Overcoming Church Conflict* (Chicago: Moody Press, 2002), 89.

9. Patrick Lencioni, *The Five Dysfunctions of a Team: A Leadership Fable* (Somerset, NJ: Jossey-Bass, 2002).

10. John Townsend and Henry Cloud, *Boundaries: When to Say Yes, How to Say No to Take Control of Your Life* (Grand Rapids, MI: Zondervan, 1992).

11. Townsend and Cloud, *Boundaries,* 88–90.

12. Jodi Detrick, *The Jesus-Hearted Woman: 10 Leadership Qualities for Enduring and Endearing Influence* (Springfield, MO: Influence Resources, 2013), 48.

13. Townsend and Cloud, *Boundaries,* 236.

14. The Do's and Don'ts of grief were adapted from these sources: Christi Foster, "Life Support for the Grieving Mother: Applying CPR in Times of Tragedy." Women.ag.org. National Women's Department, General Council Assemblies of God. Accessed November 25, 2013. <http://women.ag.org/Equipping_display. aspx?id=1729&Langtype=1033>; "Supporting a Grieving Person: Helping Others Through Grief, Loss, and Bereavement." Helpguide. org: A Trusted Non-Profit Resource. Helpguide.org International. Accessed November 25, 2013. <http://www.helpguide.org/mental/ helping_grieving.htm#online>; Bev Hislop, *Shepherding Women in Pain: Real Women, Real Issues, and What You Need to Know to Truly Help* (Chicago: Moody Publishers, 2010.).

15. Andy Stanley, *Enemies of the Heart: Breaking Free from the Four Emotions That Control You* (Colorado Springs: Multnomah Books, 2011), 176.

About the Author

. . .

Kerry Clarensau is the Director of a national Christian women's organization with over 340,000 members. She is a credentialed minister, a mentor, and an international speaker. A prolific writer, she creates training materials and Internet resources for ministry to women and is the author of *Secrets: Transforming Your Life and Marriage, Love Revealed,* and *Redeemed.*

Kerry and her husband, Mike, have two sons, Tyler and Blake; a daughter-in-law, Katie; and two granddaughters, Molly Jayne and Lennon Mae.

To learn more about Kerry, visit www.kerryclarensau.com. You can follow her on Twitter: @kerryclarensau; Facebook: kerry.clarensau; and Pinterest: kerry_clarensau.

Other Titles by Kerry Clarensau

• • •

Secrets: Transforming Your Life and Marriage

Secrets: Transforming Your Life and Marriage DVD and CDROM

Secretos: Transforme su vida y su matrimonio

Redeemed!: Embracing a Transformed Life

Redeemed!: Embracing a Transformed Life DVD

¡Redimida!

¡Redimida! DVD

Love Revealed: Experiencing God's Authentic Love

El Amor Revelado: Experimente el genuino amor de Dios

The Love Revealed Challenge: 45 Days to Discovering God's Authentic Love

Desafío el Amor Revelado: 45 días para descubrir el genuino amor de Dios

• • •

For more information about these resources
please visit www.influenceresources.com